KU-156-214

Contents

SURVIVING
at work

The **Life Quality Management** series
for anyone balancing the needs of a
healthy lifestyle with the demands of
work. Each book can help you
improve the quality of your life, in
spite of work and its hazards.

Other titles include
Beating Stress at Work
Eating Well at Work
Staying Fit at Work

Carol Cooper

Published in 1995

Health Education Authority
Hamilton House
Mabledon Place, London WC1H 9TX

ISBN 0 7521 0166 8

A CIP catalogue record for this book is available from the British Library.

Typesetting by Type Generation Ltd.

Printed and bound in Great Britain by
Biddles Ltd, Guildford and King's Lynn

Acknowledgement

Many of the statistics relating to accidents and injuries at work, reported in this book, are from the *Health and Safety Commission Annual Report 1992/93*, and are reproduced with permission from the Controller of Her Majesty's Stationery Office.

Preface

Few days go by without a news item linking some aspect of work to ill-health. Thus we have had headlines like 'Farm workers poisoned by sheep dip', 'Cement burns builder's leg', 'Car resprayers risk brain damage', 'Heavy manual work can lead to osteoarthritis', 'Latex allergy places medics' lives at risk', 'Junior doctor drops dead after 86-hour week', 'Teleworkers have more family problems' and even 'Money can be a sickener' (a reference to nickel allergy in cashiers).

Under the circumstances, it can be easy to forget the positive aspects of work. Apart from the obvious one of generating income, work has many benefits. It gives structure to the day, provides social stimulus, enhances self-esteem and confers status and identity. "What do you do?" is often the first question asked at social gatherings. Work has a therapeutic role. Many of us know its value as a distraction from mental distress. Work is important in rehabilitating the injured, the chronically ill and psychiatric patients. Work can also be enjoyable, even, as Noël Coward put it, more fun than fun.

His near-contemporary Kipling noted that "If you don't work, you die". There is now increasing evidence that job loss is bad for mental and physical health, and that it can indeed kill. Being unemployed is thought to raise the chances of a man dying in the next 10 years by about 30 per cent. It affects family health too, increasing the risk of illness in his wife and children. Perhaps a P45 should carry a health warning.

To get the best out of our working lives, as well as produce our best, it is vital to be aware of workday hazards and to take the right steps to tackle them. I hope this book will help you to do that.

Carol Cooper

CHAPTER ONE

Occupational health

Occupational disease goes back a long way, possibly as far as the Stone Age. Prehistoric man may well have developed silicosis from making flint tools, though he left no written evidence of it. The ancient Greeks and Egyptians probably knew the hazards of mining gold, silver and lead, since these jobs were kept for convicts and slaves.

It was not until the 18th century that the Italian physician Bernardino Ramazzini published his *De Mortis Artificum*, a ground-breaking work on occupational disease which owed something to his observations of eye symptoms in cesspit workers. Nonetheless, humanitarian feelings continued to run low amongst employers, most of whom had a cavalier disregard for the effects of work on health.

The new technology introduced during the industrial revolution changed the patterns of disease. Those working in noisy factories were liable to develop boilermaker's deafness. Workers in cotton mills were often rendered breathless from byssinosis. The lubricating oil from the spinning jenny, which was rich in carcinogens, saturated the spinners' trousers and raised the incidence of cancer of the scrotum. Problems also arose from longer working hours and other social effects. In new industrial areas the accommodation was often cramped and the sanitation primitive. Sometimes whole families moved to the industrial area, but not always. When the breadwinner had to leave wife and children behind, family breakup sometimes followed.

Working conditions began to improve through the

philanthropy of individual employers, a trend which continues today. Altruism is not the only motive, however. Fit employees are more productive, and improving health at work results in decreased absence and increased output. Today, concern for employee welfare is also a matter of complying with the law, and responding to pressure from trade unions. For many firms it plays a role in enhancing corporate image.

Even today, nobody knows exactly much illness is due to work, but several statistics are worth noting.

- For 1991/92, there were 170,400 injuries to employees at work in the UK, and 297 deaths (figures from *Health and Safety Commission Annual Report 1992/93*).
- Nearly 4000 dangerous occurrences at work are reported every year. According to the Health and Safety Commission, every service sector employee can expect an average of one physical injury at work during his or her career.
- Every year there are about 6000 new claims for compensation for disablement by industrial diseases, such as pneumoconiosis (lung disease caused by inhaling various dusts) and vibration syndrome (damage from machinery such as chainsaws and pneumatic drills, usually affecting circulation in the hand).
- The Health & Safety Executive estimates that every year there are 60,000 new cases of work-related skin disease and 20,000 new cases of some form of upper limb disorder.
- According to figures from the Department of Health and Social Security (DHSS), over 30 million certified days off sick every year are due to work-related illness or injury – an average of more than one day, lost per worker per year.
- The Confederation of British Industry (CBI) estimates that industry's total costs for sickness absence, including lost production and compensation, are of the order of £13 billion

per annum, or about £12,000 for every company in the UK. Work-related illness may cost society 2–3 per cent of gross domestic product, which makes health at work everyone's concern.

SICKNESS ABSENCE

It is estimated that 750,000 people each year take time off work for what they perceive to be work-related ill-health. Unfortunately, as some have discovered, one can be dismissed for repeated absences caused by sickness, on the grounds that attendance at work has been unsatisfactory.

There are many ways of reducing sickness absence, including

- staying healthy – the main subject of this book
- getting the right help when unwell
- having a job appropriate to one's skills, interests and degree of fitness
- having support in personal crises.

THE SCOPE OF OCCUPATIONAL HEALTH

Occupational health goes well beyond the confines of health and safety at work.

Its role is to deal with the impact of health on work and the effect of work on health, so its functions include

- assessing whether a worker is fit for a particular type of work
- preventing ill-health caused by work
- educating staff and encouraging them and their families to adopt a healthier lifestyles. This can be done, for example, through policies on smoking, education about alcohol, and liaison with the catering department to provide healthy lunches.

FIT FOR WHAT? THE EFFECT OF HEALTH ON WORK

It is fairly obvious, for example, that people who drive for their living should have good eyesight. Someone with recurrent back pain would be well advised to avoid work involving heavy lifting. Also, anyone with haemophilia should not become a carpet-fitter because repeated trauma to the knee can cause bleeding into the knee joint.

There are many other physical restrictions on certain types of work, some of them subtle, and these form the rationale for pre-employment medical screening.

Pre-employment medicals

A pre-employment medical is often the first contact an employee has with occupational health. Since many new employees are fit young people, however, routine medicals for everyone tend to be unrewarding. Nowadays the trend is to use a questionnaire in combination with an interview by a nurse who also checks such things as vision and blood pressure. Only if it then appears necessary will examination by a doctor take place.

Some candidates worry about the allegiance of medical staff and may withhold certain facts, either when filling in their questionnaires or on being seen by the nurse or doctor. It is correct to think that occupational health staff work for the company, but even so they still owe a patient confidentiality. If a candidate is unfit for a job, for instance, the doctor conveys this to management in the most general terms, and will only divulge medical details with the informed consent of the prospective employee.

WHO DOES WHAT IN OCCUPATIONAL HEALTH?

The first port of call for anyone concerned about their health is, as usual, the family doctor. General practitioners (GPs) are used to dealing with everyday complaints, such as anxiety, back pain and insomnia. For many people, these are the only problems which arise from work. It is also useful if the GP has permission to liaise with the employer about preventing the recurrence of the problem, for example back pain.

The provision of occupational health in this country is uneven and largely voluntary. About a quarter of all workplaces offer some kind of occupational health service which leaves three-quarters (and about half the workforce) without even rudimentary provision. Smaller businesses tend to need occupational health services most, but are least likely to provide any.

Occupational health doctors have a role which is largely preventive. Usually trained in occupational medicine, they are normally associates or full members of the Faculty of Occupational Medicine, a branch of the Royal College of Physicians. They

- have responsibility for identifying, diagnosing and treating occupational disease
- medically examine and advise individual employees when needed
- advise on fitness for work
- help the company develop policies on health
- help in rehabilitating employees
- monitor environmental hazards
- give advice on control measures
- may teach or do research

If there is no occupational health doctor, there may be a medical adviser, often a visiting local GP with a special interest in occupational health, though not always with special training. There are also a number of independent consultants in occupational medicine who may be called in to advise on health policy or a particular problem. Sometimes group occupational health services can provide help for a group of small to medium sized companies.

Occupational health nurses may work with an occupational health doctor or a visiting medical adviser, but are very often autonomous.

The occupational nurse

- gives advice on fitness for work
- provides health surveillance
- supervises first-aiders
- monitors ill-health trends at work
- conducts risk assessments
- gives lifestyle advice
- may provide counselling.

Designated first-aiders give emergency treatment for injuries. A first-aider must be trained by an organisation approved by the Health & Safety Executive, and has a certificate valid for 3 years, after which time a refresher course is needed (see Chapter 12 on accidents).

Occupational hygienists evaluate health hazards at work and help to keep them under control. Hygienists are often brought in as consultants to advise on such things as the safety of manufacturing processes. They may also monitor dust, fumes and ventilation systems.

Ergonomists are discussed in Chapter 2.

Other professionals such as toxicologists and safety engineers, who work behind the scenes, are involved in occupational health departments. More visible to the average employee will be some of the services a large business such as a petrochemical company or major bank may provide, for instance dental services, physiotherapy and chiropody.

HEALTH & SAFETY LEGISLATION

The main act covering the health of the workforce is the Health and Safety at Work Act etc 1974 which covers everyone at work, whether employed or self-employed. Under this act, all employers must ensure, so far as is reasonably practicable, the health, safety and welfare at work of their employees, and of any others (such as visitors and the local community) who may be affected by the work.

Employers are specifically responsible for
● assessing hazards in the workplace
● removing or controlling the risks
● monitoring control measures to make sure they work
● providing employees with appropriate information and training

Regulations made under the act cover a range of particular hazards, such as visual display units, manual handling, personal protective equipment and the control of hazardous substances.

In 1986, the Reporting of Industrial Diseases and Dangerous Occurrence Regulations (RIDDOR) were introduced. Under these regulations
● all accidents at work causing death or serious injury must be reported promptly to the Health & Safety Executive (HSE)
● all injuries at work leading to more than 3 days absence must also be reported to the HSE
● 'close calls' and near misses, such as fires and explosions, must also be reported even if no one was hurt
● all 'prescribed' occupational diseases must be reported

There is a long list of these, which include work-related hearing loss, lead poisoning, occupational asthma and vibration white finger (a condition which can be caused by habitual work with pneumatic drills).

Who enforces it?

Health and safety at work is enforced by inspectors from the HSE, and by Environmental Health Officers from the local authority. Local authorities are responsible for shops, hotels and offices, while the HSE deals with most of the rest.

The Health & Safety Executive (HSE) is an organisation set up as a result of the Health and Safety at Work etc Act. Apart from its role in enforcing legislation and monitoring hazards, it also exists to develop occupational health policy.

HSE inspectors have powers to visit workplaces and carry out tests (which may include taking photographs and samples) to determine compliance with the law. Inspectors can

● give informal advice and information to an employer
● serve improvement notices or prohibition notices which specify measures to control health and safety hazards. In some cases, work has to be suspended until remedial action is seen to have been taken. (One recent example is that of a Birmingham laboratory working with carcinogenic viruses. Even though the viruses were 'disabled', the laboratory was shut down in December 1993 by a prohibition notice because of possible shortcomings in safety precautions.)
● prosecute employers who fail to comply with the law

If successful, a court action usually results in a company paying a fine. Many critics, however, believe fines to be insufficient deterrents. It might be more effective to institute criminal proceedings and hold company directors personally liable for serious breaches of the law, or when an employee has been killed at work. The Law Commission is seeking changes in the law to make it easier to charge company directors with manslaughter when this seems appropriate.

There are over 1500 HSE inspectors covering areas as diverse as factory work, nuclear installations, mines, quarries, railways, agriculture and offshore work. However, with 24 million people in employment in over one million workplaces, inspectors cannot inspect all premises. The HSE budget has been cut for 1994/95, so the work of the inspectorate will become even more of a challenge.

The Employment Medical Advisory Service (EMAS) is a branch of the HSE, staffed by doctors and nurses trained in occupational health. EMAS has a wide range of duties including
- advising workers and their doctors (in confidence) on work-related illness.
- helping employees and industry manage health problems.
- advising trade unions.
- investigating new hazards.
- appointing doctors to undertake statutory medicals to comply with specific legislation.

WORRIED ABOUT YOUR HEALTH AT WORK?

If so, get more information by
- checking back with any handbooks or other information your employer gave you
- contacting your company's occupational health department, if there is one
- talking to your firm's safety officer or your supervisor
- asking EMAS (the service is confidential). Contact EMAS via your nearest HSE office

If you have any symptoms you suspect are related to your work
- see your occupational health doctor or nurse
- see your GP as well. Tell the doctor as much as possible about your work. Saying you are an internal auditor or tea-bag shredder may not convey as much to someone else as it does to you.

CHAPTER TWO

Ergonomics

Ergonomics is the study of work and machinery from a human point of view, the aim being to adapt the workplace to those who have to use it.

Like rock and roll, ergonomics is a post-war phenomenon. Ergonomics grew from the realisation that much of the weaponry developed for World War II failed in the job it aimed to do. Unaware of human limitations, designers had created a number of devices that were too unwieldy or awkward to use.

At first, ergonomics was mainly concerned with the physical environment, such as the height of worktops and the design of seating. Nowadays its scope includes

- work posture
- prevention of back pain
- visual display unit (VDU) workstation design
- prevention of repetitive strain injury
- architecture
- training
- software design
- aspects of accident prevention
- organisation of shiftwork
- workload and stress

In the decades during which ergonomics has blossomed, the science has contributed to a holistic approach to work. There is now a wealth of guidelines on optimum working conditions for different types of job. Some might even say there are too many, and less caring employers may be tempted to ignore them all.

THE WORK OF ERGONOMISTS

Ergonomists are often engaged by a company on a consultancy basis. An ergonomist might
- seek the views of staff
- analyse human movement around the workplace
- study office layout and workstations
- measure noise, humidity, temperature and lighting
- check software for clarity
- analyse accidents

Why are they needed?

A business needs an ergonomist no more than an individual needs to have his feet measured. It is possible, and often cheaper, to get a pair of shoes which almost fit. But wearing them in is a painful process.

Employing an ergonomist and putting into effect the changes he or she suggests can be expensive, but they are worthwhile in the long run. Work which is ergonomically unsound is generally less productive and less healthy, and contributes to poor employer–employee relations.

COULD YOUR WORK BENEFIT?

See how many of the following apply to you.
- Is your office about to be altered?
- Have you just moved to a new post?
- Is your work repetitive, either physically or mentally?
- Do you sit (or stand) for much of the day?
- Do you find it necessary to have frequent breaks?
- Do you enjoy your job, but develop aches and pains after a day's work? (If they are in the legs, your seat may be the wrong height; pain in the back may be caused by your seat,

desk or lifting; painful eyes could be affected by VDU screen design or office lighting.)

- Do you keep having the same type of injury or accident? (This may range from inadvertently keying in the wrong symbols to bumping into the same corner of a desk.)
- Do you avoid protective clothing or equipment because it is uncomfortable or inconvenient?
- Are you well below or above average height or weight?

If any of these points apply to you, your workplace may benefit from an ergonomic approach. The first step is to discuss it with management. It is helpful to have thought about the problem before bringing it to your employer's attention, and it is more impressive too.

OFFICE SEATING

One could select chairs in the same way as Goldilocks, trying them out until you find one which is just right. Like bears, people differ, but there are general requirements which a glance at many offices would suggest are often ignored.

- The seat must be the right depth for the user. Too short is uncomfortable. Too deep and the edge digs into the back of the knee.
- It must be the right height. Your legs should neither dangle nor hit the underside of the desk.
- Support in the lumbar area is a must. Support elsewhere in the back, higher or lower, is optional.
- The seat should tilt forwards slightly so that the lumbar spine is kept slightly curved (feel the hollow above the small of the back). About 10 degrees is optimal. More leads to slipping forward, especially in a skirt.
- Arm rests are useful when getting up from a chair, are nice to

lean on when talking to people and also look good. But they can get in the way of the desk and stop the user from pushing the chair in close enough.

● The value of castors is debatable. They can make the chair too mobile, but are useful if the area is carpeted since friction makes chairs more difficult to move.

● The seat should face the work. It is fashionable for clients to sit beside your desk so you can talk to them in a 'non-confrontational' way. But sitting asymmetrically can lead to back pain.

Adjustable seats such as the gas lift type are best. Job-sharers in particular should make a point of adjusting the seat whenever someone else has used it.

THE DESK

Although seating is often deficient and may need replacing, desks are usually more satisfactory. This is just as well, since a desk is often a treasured status symbol as well as a surface to work on.

● Desks may look more impressive face on, but are best positioned at 90 degrees to windows, or failing that some other angle, but not parallel.

● The desk must be large enough, especially now that computers often occupy part of it and the other stuff has not gone away. The front edge should be smooth.

● The desk should be high enough to accommodate the knees comfortably, crossed if necessary. While small people can raise the seat and ask for a footrest, tall people have a problem unless desk height is adjustable (it rarely is).

● For computing, the keyboard should be at elbow height, while for writing the desk should be at elbow height. There may be conflict here, even with slim keyboards.

● Mess creates stress. Desks should be organised so that immediate work is straight ahead and in such a way that you do not knock over the pencils every time you need a paperclip. Nothing essential should be on the far corners of the desk (these are best kept for family photos). The phone (and fax) should be accessible, since stretching for them can be hard work.

● Drawers should be easy to open. If files are often needed from a cabinet, it is better to position it a few steps away rather than adjacent to the desk (where you may be tempted to over-stretch or twist to reach it).

COMPUTING

● Screens should be positioned to be in the line of sight, or about 15–30 degrees below it. The recommended distance is 50–75 cm from the eyes and obviously what is on the screen must be legible at this distance, taking into account the eyesight of the user.

● The screen itself should be easy to read. Black letters on a white background (as in printed matter) are usually easier to see, but the reverse is true in poor light. Glare from light sources should be minimal.

● Workers should not have to struggle to keep up with technology nor be driven up the wall by slow response times to commands. Software should be friendly and comprehensive.

See Chapter 9 for the possible health hazards from VDUs and ways of preventing them.

LIGHTING

Eyes run on light – a fact which is not widely appreciated. Office lighting should fulfil three main requirements

- there must be enough of it
- it must come from the right direction
- it should be even, without flicker

Normal office illumination is far brighter than the average sitting room. However, extreme brightness is both unnecessary and uncomfortable. As for watching television, using a VDU demands lower levels of ambient light.

Task lighting should not be too close to the line of sight, and conventionally it should come from the opposite side to the hand used for writing. There should be a reasonable degree of contrast between the immediate work area and the desk or table top on which it rests. The walls should not reflect too much light – gloss paint on walls is a bad idea.

Flickering strip lights are irritating. Even 'invisible' flicker can annoy and may cause headaches and eye symptoms. These can be avoided by changing the type of light fitting.

Almost everyone appreciates windows. Windowless offices are stressful and provide no view – the two facts may be related. In Japan, one solution to soul-less office environments is to install fake windows which provide a selection of 'views' and landscapes as well as avoid the glare and heat loss (or gain) from real windows.

CHAPTER THREE

Stress

Like happiness, stress is easy to recognise but hard to measure. That is one reason why it does not always figure prominently in scientific work. In the eyes of the average person, however, stress is public enemy number one, responsible for much ill health and most cases of heart disease.

According to research conducted for the Confederation of British Industry (CBI), three in every five companies now design jobs and training specifically to alleviate stress. Just as well, since employees have taken their employers to court for stress-related ills.

Stress has become an overused word, almost a kind of shorthand. "I'm really stressed" (or "stressed out") may mean "I want you to know that things are going badly and I'm not coping all that well. It's too complicated to go into it and besides you wouldn't have the time to listen".

WHAT IS STRESS?

There are two main ways to think of stress.
- It can be seen, as in GCSE level physics, as a force acting on an individual.
- It may be the change within an individual as a result of outside pressure. In terms of physics, this is actually strain, not stress, but it is the meaning most often accepted by psychologists and doctors – even if it cannot be measured as easily as one can measure changes in a piece of elastic.

Clearly some external pressure is beneficial and can improve individual performance for example, in the case of someone studying for an exam, or even a mouse in a laboratory. It is when pressure exceeds the capacity of that person to cope with it that problems can result. Professor Cary Cooper, professor of organizational psychology at the University of Manchester Institute of Science and Technology, describes a stress equation:

$$\text{life stress} + \text{work stress} + \text{individual vulnerability} = \text{stress symptoms.}$$

Individual vulnerability can change over the years.

As for studying the effects of stress, a convenient compromise is that whenever psycho-social events or conditions appear to be related to physical ill-health, we call the symptoms or the illness stress-related. On this basis, some 30–40 per cent of all sickness absence from work has been estimated to be stress related. The cost to business has been reckoned to be about £7 billion a year.

THE EFFECTS OF STRESS

A variety of symptoms can be stress-related. Perhaps you feel
● irritable ● sad or tearful ● angry ● unable to cope ● little interest in life ● little interest in others ● anxious or afraid ● indecisive ● unable to show your feelings ● a failure ● ugly ● you hate yourself
Or maybe you suffer from some of these
● indigestion ● intermittent constipation/diarrhoea ● loss of appetite. ● tiredness ● headaches ● insomnia ● palpitations ● passing water often ● impotence ● nervous twitches ● nail biting ● drinking too much ● taking illicit drugs

Many of these symptoms have other possible causes. For instance heart disease can cause palpitations, colitis can cause diarrhoea, and one usually feels weepy and worthless in depression.

In addition, some individuals under stress believe they have physical disease. This is partly because physical conditions are more acceptable than emotional ill-health. However, stress is undoubtedly a factor in a variety of physical conditions, such as ● heart disease ● high blood pressure ● migraine ● asthma ● peptic ulcer ● skin disorders (e.g. eczema, acne, psoriasis) ● lowered immunity to infection

The British Heart Foundation agrees stress is important in heart disease. There are even psychological treatments (or angina management programmes) which incorporate yoga, relaxation and pain management techniques and which can help angina patients while waiting for heart bypass surgery.

The role of stress in cancer is contentious, though doctors have long known that adverse life events, for want of a better term, seem to be linked with relapses of various malignancies.

HOW DOES STRESS INFLUENCE HEALTH?

Nobody really knows, but there are possible physiological pathways whereby stress could affect health. We know for instance that individuals under stress secrete higher quantities of the hormones adrenalin and noradrenalin from their adrenal glands. The short-term effects are known as the 'fight or flight reaction' (or the stress response). The reaction helps an individual respond to attack by ● increasing pulse rate ● raising blood pressure ● mobilising glycogen from the liver to raise blood glucose ● dilating the pupils ● breathing faster

Other changes include tense muscles, and increased platelet stickiness leading to faster clotting. This is useful for controlling bleeding if an adversary sticks a knife into you, but it is of less benefit when the adversary is a packed appointments book or a difficult colleague.

It is easy to imagine how these changes might, in the long term, lead to heart disease, though nothing is so far proven. Ill-health may not even be caused by stress *per se* but rather by behavioural changes associated with stressful events, for instance, eating badly and exercising less.

WHO SUFFERS FROM STRESS?

Anyone can suffer from stress at work, though there are several important factors including ● personality ● status at work ● control over work conditions ● conflict between home and work

Traditionally it is the type A personality who becomes stressed, according to US cardiologists Mayer Freedman and Ray Rosenbaum who propounded their theories on heart disease and personality about three decades ago. The Type A person is aggressive, competitive, impatient and irritable. The Type B person is not necessarily less of an achiever, but is more laid-back and less rushed, rather like the person Kipling may have had in mind when he penned his poem *If*.

Most people have heard of types A and B and can accept their different propensities to stress symptoms. Less often publicised is that stress is not the exclusive province of executives and middle managers; in fact those in more lowly posts are more likely to suffer stress-related symptoms. Some years ago, Professor Michael Marmot's Whitehall study of male civil servants aged 40 to 64 found that those in the lowest grades (such as messengers) had three times the mortality of men in the highest (administrative) grade.

True, messengers smoked more, had higher blood pressures, and were more likely to be diabetic. But even taking these characteristics into account did not fully explain the difference. Perhaps the clues lie in the messengers' unsatisfying work, underuse of their skills, or lack of control over their work.

These factors, especially that of control over work, have received more attention lately, and it is now clear that being in a non-executive or non-decision making position is more stressful. Observations of doctors following a new 'contract' – unilaterally imposed on GPs in 1990 by the Department of Health - suggest that having to cope with change without being able to influence it is a potent stressor.

Another important factor is conflict between work and life outside the workplace. This can affect almost anyone, but, as many working women have discovered, it is commonly found in parents, especially if they have heavy domestic duties, unsatisfactory childcare arrangements or poor support from their partner.

Similarly, employees with chronic illnesses, such as arthritis, are often in conflict because they may want to work but may suffer more physical pain if they do too much.

Clearly preventing stress may require action in many areas, such as ● company organisation ● individual behaviour ● attitudes of society.

BURN-OUT

This is the term used to describe the physical and mental exhaustion which is the end-product of job stress. Although no profession is entirely immune, burn-out tends to affect those in caring professions, such as nursing, medicine and counselling. Perhaps this is because these people often think of themselves as being indispensable.

Usual symptoms include ● loss of sense of humour ● emotional withdrawal at work and at home ● lack of interest in work ● hostility to others ● physical symptoms (e.g. insomnia) ● exhaustion, even when doing things one wants to do

Problems can be avoided if stress is tackled early and the problem is shared. People at high risk of burn-out find this difficult to do.

COPING WITH STRESS

Handling pressure at work and staving off the symptoms of stress is not always easy, but several coping skills are worth practising.

● Try to be more realistic with your plans. Will what you are struggling so hard with today matter in 5 years from now? Or even 1 year? Abandon unimportant tasks and prioritise what needs to be done.

● Do not create unnecessary deadlines for yourself or get yourself into a corner. Delegate more.

● Learn to say "No", in an assertive rather than aggressive way. If you are bad at standing up for your rights without alienating others, consider assertiveness training.

● Consciously slow yourself down. Eat more slowly and drive more slowly (classical music on the car radio can help). Do not try to talk all the time. Silence is not intrinsically bad. It can even have a positive effect by making what you do say seem more important.

● Learn to relax. You may benefit from a relaxation course, either with a teacher or from an audio cassette.

● Look after yourself. make sure you exercise, eat well, cut down on drink and get enough sleep. Just as importantly, make time just for yourself to do something you enjoy every day.

● Make the most of support from family, friends and colleagues.

● Tackle symptoms early. They are trying to tell you something.

IF YOU ARE SUFFERING FROM STRESS

- Accept that suffering from stress is not being a failure.
- Tell your employer about the areas of work which are especially stressful. There is sometimes a ready solution.
- Use your company's services, such as occupational health and stress counselling, which many large firms now provide.
- See your doctor. Your GP may be able to help directly, refer you to a psychologist, and/or liaise with the occupational health department. You may benefit from yoga, transcendental meditation, or time management.
- You could find it helpful to contact your trade union. Some workers have found it valuable to form their own informal workshops, with the aim of supporting each other and finding solutions to common work stress problems.

INSOMNIA

About a third of people suffer from inability to sleep, which is often a stress-related symptom. Sleeping pills are only ever a temporary help, because they are habit-forming and they also become less effective with time.

'Sleep hygiene' is the term used for general advice which can improve sleep:

- Avoid coffee, tea and caffeine-containing soft drinks in the evening, say from 6 p.m. onwards.
- Avoid excess alcohol. It helps sleep to begin with, but you may wake up more in the night.
- Light carbohydrate snacks (e.g. a bowl of cereal) and hot milky drinks taken shortly before bedtime can help.
- Take enough exercise during the day (see Chapter 15 on exercise).

- 'Debrief' before bedtime by setting aside 15 minutes for thinking about your problems. Write them down if it helps.

- Try to unwind with a pleasant routine, such as a warm bath or soft music. Specific relaxation techniques are very helpful. If you do not know any, just breathe in and out deeply and slowly. Or try to contract and then let go of each of your muscles in turn.

- Use your bed only for sleep and sex – not for reading, working or watching television.

- Go to bed only when you are tired.

- Banish all intrusive thoughts. Repeating something dull can help. For example, count sheep or repeat a neutral word like 'the'.

- If you fail to nod off within 20 minutes, do not worry about it. Either get up and do something in another room until you are really sleepy, or decide that you are prepared to put up with being awake. At least your body is resting when you are lying in bed.

- You cannot force yourself to sleep, but if all else fails, you may succeed by forcing yourself to stay awake. Keep your eyes open as long as you can – before long, they will invariably shut!

- Daytime naps spoil sleep patterns, so do not have naps unless they are essential, for instance to maintain alertness later for a vital or hazardous task (see Chapter 14 on shiftwork).

- If depression, pain, or other symptoms are the cause of your insomnia, get help.

TENSION HEADACHE

This is a common complaint. It is estimated that about 97 per cent of headaches are caused by tension, which is physical as much as mental. Important causative factors are prolonged concentration, tense neck muscles, poor posture or seating and possibly stuffy surroundings and flickering lights.

A tension headache can feel like ● a band around the head ● crushing pain ● throbbing ● pressure behind the eyes

It may go on for days and, unlike the headache associated with brain tumours, is usually worse in the evening. Sometimes it only comes on after work or at weekends.

This type of headache responds poorly to medicines, but it is worth trying simple analgesics, such as aspirin or paracetamol. In theory, muscle relaxants are more helpful, but in practice they are often habit-forming. You may succeed in relaxing muscles with an ice-pack, neck massage or relaxation training instead.

Measures to reduce stress and prevent tension headache are also important. At work, take breaks and do something else for a few minutes, outside if you can. If you cannot break off from work, at least focus on distant objects from time to time and move your head about to reduce strain on neck muscles. However hard you are working, try not to take worries home.

On rare occasions, headache is a symptom of serious disease, especially if it comes on violently or is associated with unusual symptoms, such as weakness in part of the body, clumsiness, double vision or fits.

CHAPTER FOUR

Work skills and satisfaction

WORK SKILLS

Skills needed at work vary from job to job, but some are common to most types of work. Maximising your potential in such areas can help you perform better and enjoy work more.

Finding things

If you do not know where something is, it clearly helps to know what it looks like (e.g. big, shiny, blue spine with red lettering). The use of colour on files is an obvious aid.

It is even better to keep things in the right place, which is a good justification for tidiness. "I know it looks a mess", some say of the avalanche of papers in front of them, "but I know where everything is". This is rarely true. A cluttered desk certainly fosters an impression of industry, but the truth is that mess creates stress.

Some firms have clear-desk policies so that everything is put away every evening. Apart from making it easier to keep the desk clean, it is also physically easier to work at a tidy desk. The work is also more productive because there are fewer visual distractions. When organising your desk, keep much needed things accessible and, if possible, in the order in which they are used.

Good housekeeping is hard for those who are not naturally

tidy, but it is worth making an effort to clear your desk regularly, say at the end of every week so that you start on Monday knowing where you are.

Memory

If you are helped by seeing a pattern or using a mnemonic, fine. Most of us only remember that dromedaries have one hump from seeing a letter D on its side.

Try to cut down on interruptions when you are committing material to memory. Do not bother to remember what you could read instead. Write it down, preferably on something that will not go astray.

Avoid taxing other people's memories with long-winded instructions and speeches loaded with subordinate clauses. Their attention may trail off long before you get to the main verb of the sentence.

Concentration

Many factors adversely affect concentration, for instance

- lack of sleep
- time of day
- physical discomfort
- ill-health
- emotional conflict
- bad relations at work
- work overload
- interruptions

It was in 1890 when the 84-hour week at blast furnaces was reduced, reducing accidents and absenteeism. Yet the effects of lack of sleep on concentration and performance are only now being paid proper attention. Some have recently suggested that major accidents, such as the Exxon Valdez oil spill, the Clapham rail disaster and the explosion at the Chernobyl power plant may have been caused by lack of sleep. The message is – get enough sleep – and do not make crucial decisions when you are not alert.

It is not clear why some people are larks (more awake in the morning) and others are owls (more awake at night). There is a preponderance of morning types among older people, and perhaps among women too. The causes are probably a combination of nature and nurture. It is known that even in their 30s, morning people suffer significant lapses after lunch. If you are a morning type, make the most of that time of day by using it for high priority work, delicate negotiations, and reading through difficult material.

A slight afternoon dip in alertness is usual and often attributed to blood flow being diverted to the gut to aid the digestion of lunch. However, firm evidence is lacking, and similar symptoms occur even if lunch is missed. It is possible that early afternoon is simply the body's natural siesta time, as is well known in countries where no attempt is made to fight it.

It has now been shown that short naps in the day can make up for a certain amount of sleep deficit. Although cat-napping may later spoil night-time sleep, taking a nap can make all the difference to concentration and decision-making on a day when one has not had enough sleep the night before.

Taking work home

'Carry-over' is the term used for the effect work has on home life. If you feel good about your work, or have achieved something worthwhile, carry-over can be positive, enhancing home life and relationships. Carry-over is negative when work is stressful, there is too much of it, or it is unsatisfying in other ways.

Most work is mentally taxing, even when it does not appear to be. Boring or repetitive work (the traditional assembly line job) requires little energy but may result in the same types of problems as more 'stressful' high-powered jobs. Work underload, as it has been described, can be associated with physical ill-health, according to some psychologists. It can also lead to higher absenteeism, which is not necessarily the same thing.

Physically taking work home in the form of a bulging briefcase or a laptop computer may be an added stressor. Sometimes it has to be done, for example when deadlines have to be met, childcare arrangements have broken down or there are transport difficulties. If you must do this

- try to set aside a time and place in your home to do the work
- give yourself a suitable reward for it
- get it out of your system before going to bed (e.g. by having a warm bath and/or jotting down problems instead of mulling over them all night)

HOW SATISFYING IS YOUR JOB?

Many of the items in this quiz are factors affecting occupational stress and mental health. Be as honest as you can. The aim is to focus on some aspects of your work and thereby suggest ways of improving it. Make a note of your answers and add up your score at the end.

1. **Is your job appropriate to your level of skill?**
   a) more or less
   b) above my head
   c) an insult to my intelligence

2. **Would you describe your workload as**
   a) too high
   b) too low
   c) usually about right, but it varies?

---

3   Do you meet lots of people at work?
   a) not usually
   b) yes
   c) yes but they're a load of idiots

4   Promotion prospects are
   a) good
   b) poor
   c) who knows? Nobody stays that long

5   Do you look forward to Monday mornings?
   a) definitely not
   b) sort of
   c) I am slightly apprehensive, but this wears off quickly

6   Who plans your working day?
   a) I do
   b) it is all mapped out for me
   c) in theory I am my own boss but in practice there
   are too many interruptions

7   Do you feel in control of important decisions?
   a) mostly
   b) sometimes
   c) are you kidding? They use the mushroom
   management style here

8   The pay is
   a) good
   b) hopeless
   c) money for old rope
   d) not brilliant, but there is a pay review soon

9   The work
   a) is varied

b) could be done standing on my head

c) would be better if I could occasionally swap tasks with others

10 You have been trained
    a) to about the right level
    b) I was thrown in the deep end
    c) I am fully trained but someone is still breathing down my neck

11 Your attitude to delegating is
    a) if you want something done, you have to do it yourself
    b) I have fairly good support
    c) I would love to delegate, but to whom?

12 You get feedback
    a) always
    b) occasionally
    c) when things go wrong

13 As far as role boundaries go
    a) I know what I am supposed to do
    b) I have recently been promoted and am not sure what is expected of me
    c) I am too busy to think of such things

14 Your employer could be described as
    a) caring
    b) fair
    c) couldn't care less

15 As for the importance of your work
    a) it is socially significant – I help others
    b) it matters to the company and clients/customers

    c) it matters to me

    d) I doubt it makes any difference to anyone

16 When you get home, you feel

    a) tired but happy

    b) relieved

    c) ready for the undertaker

Score

1 a) 3 b) 1 c) 2	9 a) 3 b) 1 c) 2
2 a) 2 b) 1 c) 3	10 a) 3 b) 1 c) 1
3 a) 1 b) 3 c) 2	11 a) 1 b) 3 c) 2
4 a) 3 b) 1 c) 2	12 a) 3 b) 2 c) 1
5 a) 1 b) 2 c) 3	13 a) 3 b) 1 c) 2
6 a) 3 b) 1 c) 2	14 a) 3 b) 3 c) 1
7 a) 3 b) 2 c) 1	15 a) 3 b) 3 c) 3 d) 1
8 a) 4 b) 1 c) 2 d) 3	16 a) 3 b) 1 c) 1

Analysis

Under 22 points: You are in a cul-de-sac and are unlikely to be happy if you stay long in this job. But it may be acceptable as long as you are doing it for a limited time.

22 to 32 points: You do not seem to be intellectually or emotionally fulfilled here. The work may be unpromising but perhaps you can do something about it, including perhaps re-examining some of your attitudes.

33 points or more: Your job is probably as rewarding as any and better than many. There may be the occasional hitches, but do not make any hasty moves.

CHAPTER FIVE

Attitudes at work – bullying and harassment

The workplace is an area where normal rules of play seem to have been suspended. People behave differently at work – often worse than at home, though occasionally better. A workaholic friend once confided she tried to be as nice to her own family as she was to colleagues and clients – she found it surprisingly hard, but concluded it was well worth doing.

Our behaviour at work is not the same towards everyone. Many people are perfectly civilised with some people, but not with others. The office is not a level playing-field, as is obvious from the way some individuals treat those who differ from them in status, class, education, race, creed or gender.

HOW DO YOU BEHAVE AT WORK?

Which of these answers most closely reflects how you behave at work? Make a note of your answers and then add up your score at the end.

1 **Do you thank staff for cooperating with you?**
   a) often
   b) occasionally
   c) almost never

2 **Do you appreciate their new ideas even when you do not go along with them?**
   a) often

---

b) occasionally

c) almost never

3 **Do you tell lies to avoid telling the truth?**

a) often

b) occasionally

c) almost never

4 **Do you ask workmates about their families?**

a) often

b) occasionally

c) almost never

5 **Do you shout or use bad language to make a point?**

a) often

b) occasionally

c) almost never

6 **Do you hand out work to staff just as they are hoping to go home?**

a) often

b) occasionally

c) almost never

7 **Do you bad-mouth workmates or spread gossip and rumour?**

a) often

b) occasionally

c) almost never

8 **Do you use memos or e-mail to avoid speaking to someone – especially when you have something unpleasant to say?**

a) often

b) occasionally

c) almost never

9 **Do you try to appear important by talking for your boss?**
   a) **often**
   b) **occasionally**
   c) **almost never**

10 **Do you treat colleagues as you would like them to treat you?**
   a) **often**
   b) **occasionally**
   c) **almost never**

Score

1 a) 2 b) 1 c) 0	6 a) 0 b) 1 c) 2
2 a) 2 b) 1 c) 0	7 a) 0 b) 1 c) 2
3 a) 0 b) 1 c) 2	8 a) 0 b) 1 c) 2
4 a) 2 b) 1 c) 0	9 a) 0 b) 1 c) 2
5 a) 0 b) 1 c) 2	10 a) 2 b) 1 c) 0

Analysis

0 to 7 points: People do things for you because they are frightened, not because you make them want to do them. Are you perhaps a tin god or workplace bully? There is no law against this behaviour, but it may be worth mending your ways before heads roll (one of which could be yours).

8 to 15 points: Your manners are fairly normal, which is not saying much. Being a little more aware of colleagues' needs and feelings might be appreciated – it can be done without sounding ingratiating.

16 or more points: Pat yourself on the back – you are almost too good to be true. Do not be considerate towards others at the expense of your own well being.

SEXUAL HARASSMENT

Harassment affects the working lives of many women. Some speak out and tell their employer and may even take the problem to court. But others silently endure escalating harasssment until it interferes with their social and family lives.

Sexual harassment can occur at any level in an organisation, but it is when the harasser is in a more senior position that it is most difficult to stop. Until recently, victims have tended to put up and shut up, or else resign.

Unlike bullying, sexual harassment is illegal. A landmark case in 1986, after laboratory technician Jean Porcelli complained of harassment by two male colleagues, established sexual harassment as discrimination under the Sex Discrimination Act 1975. Under the Act, it is illegal to discriminate against a woman by treating her less well than one would treat a man.

Women sometimes harass men. Surveys suggest a significant proportion of men may have been sexually harassed, though less often than women, for the simple reason that fewer women are in positions of power. When they are, they are usually too careful to put a foot wrong.

Other groups are also victimised. Harassment can be homophobic, or racist, and all forms are just as serious. Much of this chapter applies to all types of harassment.

WHAT EXACTLY IS HARASSMENT?

Harassment means different things to different people. Which of the following do you think constitute sexual harassment?
- placing your hand on a female colleague's knee
- propositioning the temporary typist over the photocopier
- forcing yourself on colleagues or employees
- offering promotion in return for sexual favours, even in jest

● rude gestures
● displaying newspaper pictures of nude women on the office wall
● making comments to women, such as "Wrong time of the month, is it?"
● staring hard or visually undressing a colleague
● patting your secretary's head
● telling sexual or racial jokes and then mocking those who do not find them funny
● making gender generalisations (e.g. about driving, making coffee or getting socks darned)
● calling women "Dear" and men "Sir"
● expecting your secretary to help you with your Christmas shopping
● remarks such as "Gosh, you are independent, aren't you?"

Most people would consider the first four examples to be harassment, but there is often disagreement about the others. However, all of them constitute sexual harassment.

Any unwanted act or comment of a sexual or personal nature is harassment, so clearly the definition covers a huge spectrum of behaviour. The key is how that behaviour is perceived by the other party. If the recipient feels uncomfortable, embarrassed or degraded, it is sexual harassment. Sexual harassment is therefore a one-sided business, unlike chatting someone up, for instance.

Interestingly, according to most dictionaries harassment is a long-term, repeated or continuous process of being pestered or tormented. In practice it often is, but it does not have to be to qualify as harassment.

THE EFFECTS OF HARASSMENT

Sexual harassment can be a serious attack on someone's esteem. When it goes unchecked, the effects can be far-reaching, as when the victim has to change job, give up work altogether or seek psychiatric help (harassment can cause anxiety and depression). It also undermines a woman's position at work and in society.

A number of companies and institutions have now developed policies against it, and will discipline or sack harassers. However, in many other businesses (such as small firms or organisations which have been traditional male bastions) harassment is still rife and consciousness has hardly been raised at all.

WHAT TO DO IF YOU ARE SEXUALLY HARASSED

You may be able to stop harassing gestures and comments by treating them as a joke, or by turning the tables on the offender, but it takes a strong person to do that. You might also have to defend yourself against charges of harassment!

You may decide to do nothing. If you are happy doing this, and the incident was trivial, that is fine. But bear in mind that intentional harassment tends to get worse, so it may be better to act.

This is the sequence of actions to go through if you are sexually harassed.

1 Tell the offender that this behaviour is unacceptable, that you do not like it, and that it must stop. Some people are unaware that they have offended, which is why it can help to say explicitly that an incident is sexual harassment and that you could report them for it. The problem may well end here with an apology, especially if you keep your cool. You can tell the harasser in person, or by letter if you prefer. Keep a copy of your letter or note of your conversation. If you do not feel up to telling him (or her), get someone more senior than yourself to do so on your behalf. Or take someone from your trade union (if you have one) along with you to talk to the harasser.

2 Share the problem with your workmates. This will give you moral support, especially if, as often happens, they too have been victims of the same harasser.

3 Keep a detailed log of each incident of harassment along with any written evidence (do not throw any away in disgust!).

4 Report the harasser to management and to your union. State the facts fully and calmly. You will elicit a more constructive response if you avoid losing your temper, swearing or launching into a tirade against the opposite sex. Join a trade union if you have not already done so. Some now provide counsellors to help those who have been harassed. A few companies also provide help. But do not allow yourself to be treated as if you are at fault, for instance, seeing a psychologist to help you accept the situation.

5 Consider contacting a Citizen's Advice Bureau (in the telephone book or Thomson's local telephone directory) or the Equal Opportunities Commission (EOC). The EOC can give general advice over the telephone, and in some instances it will take up cases, but only unusual ones which raise fresh issues or break new ground.

6 Take your case to an industrial tribunal, especially if you left your work on account of harassment or were sacked for complaining about it. Get advice from the EOC, or from a solicitor with this type of experience. Incidentally, you must apply to a tribunal within 3 months of the last incident of harassment.

7 Consider going to the High Court or County Court. But remember that going to law can be draining, financially and emotionally, even if you qualify for legal aid.

DRESSING FOR WORK

No woman ever 'asks for' harassment, and the assumption that she does can be emotionally damaging. If you complain about sexual harassment to management or a tribunal, you should not be asked about your personal life, sexual predilections or what you wear to work.

It should not matter one bit what a woman wears for work. Realists, however, agree that it does, just as physicists agree that for every action there is an equal and opposite reaction.

Appearance is part of our body language, and some forms of dress reinforce sexual stereotypes. It may be a seriously unfashionable view, but consider this anyway.

- It is unreasonable to exhibit acres of flesh and expect colleagues at a meeting to find other places to rest their eyes.
- If you do not want people to get the wrong message, do not send out the wrong signals.
- Women who want to be taken seriously take themselves seriously too.

GUIDELINES FOR MEN

Since you never know exactly how someone will take something until it is too late, sexual harassment can be completely unintentional. There are no hard and fast rules to live by, but the following may help.

- Behave as well as (or better than!) you would outside work.
- Do not comment on a woman's appearance unless you know her well. It is possible to make a polite enquiry about someone who looks tired, for instance, without innuendo about late nights.
- Give up generalisations based on sexual stereotypes.
- If you have offended, say sorry – especially if you mean it. It is easier than defending your corner legally.

- Avoid emotional entanglements with your juniors.
- If you are interested in inviting a colleague out after work, do not pressurise her. Make it possible for her to refuse your invitation and still continue working in the same office as you.
- If someone complains to you about being harassed by someone else, imagine how you might feel if you were a victim. Do not ignore someone else's plight.

CHAPTER SIX

The spine and posture

Research carried out for the Confederation of British Industry reveals that 60 per cent of companies are concerned about back pain. This is not surprising, considering that at least 50 million certified days off work every year are due to back trouble. The cost in lost production, sickness benefits and treatment is estimated to be in the region of £1 billion every year.

About 80 per cent of people suffer backache at some time in their lives. Every year one person in six seeks help from their GP for back pain. Women tend to complain of back pain more than men, which may reflect the demands babies put on their mothers' bodies both before and after birth. Back pain could therefore be considered a part of the human condition, and the price of assuming the upright posture, rather than walking on all fours as our forebears did. However, problems can often be avoided.

STRUCTURE OF THE SPINE

The spine is made up of vertebrae, discs and ligaments and is supported by muscles.

Vertebrae are the individual bones of the spine. They increase in size from the top to the base of the spine; the vertebrae in the neck are the smallest and those at the base of the spine the largest.

Vertebrae are usually considered in five distinct groups. There are seven vertebrae in the neck (or cervical spine), twelve in the chest (thoracic spine), five in the lower back (lumbar spine) and two more at the very base (the sacrum is made up of five fused vertebrae and the coccyx is our small vestigial tail-bone).

Vertebrae take the weight of the body and also form a bony arch to protect the spinal cord and its emerging nerve roots.

Discs connect the vertebrae and are thought to act as shock-absorbers. Towards the back, the arch of each vertebra also articulates with the one above and below by way of two facet joints, right and left. These are tiny joints, containing fluid, just like any other joint of the body.

Each disc has a firm fibrous outer casing and a soft gel-like centre, called the nucleus pulposus. By day, water is driven out of the disc, and by night it is reabsorbed, which can make a difference of up to 1 cm between your morning and evening height.

Bending forwards tends to deform the disc, and may rupture the fibres of the outer casing, allowing the nucleus pulposus to extrude through the tear. This condition is known as a slipped disc, though it is more accurate to describe it as a prolapse or herniation of the disc centre.

Ligaments are tough bands of fibre which run from vertebra to vertebra and strengthen the spine.

Muscles are essential both to move the back and to support it. Many thick muscles (the erector spinae group) run alongside the spine. Less widely appreciated is the important role abdominal muscles play in maintaining the spine. This is one reason why pregnant women are prone to back trouble. Exercises to strengthen the spine should include exercises for the tummy area.

POSTURE

The load carried by the discs varies with position. Studies show that the least weight is taken through the spine when lying flat on one's back. Less weight is taken through the spine when standing rather than sitting. But one cannot stand all the time.

Sitting upright puts considerable pressure on the discs, which increases if you bend forward or slouch. This explains why heavy physical work is linked to back pain (ask any nurse or builder). Sedentary workers also get back trouble, especially if they sit badly or neglect their muscles.

The spine follows a gentle S-shaped curve – forwards in the lumbar and cervical areas (you can feel the hollows at the back of the neck and the lower back, especially when lying down). It is important to preserve this curve even when sitting. Support in the lumbar area of a seat – whether it is part of the seat or you put a cushion behind you – can help to maintain healthy posture.

Many people find that slumping forwards in a chair is more comfortable than sitting up straight. This is because it requires less muscle effort. But it puts more pressure on the discs and can lead to back trouble later.

Good posture should start early in life. Parental exhortations to sit up straight are no bad thing since some back problems in adulthood are related to bad habits formed as a child.

WHAT GOES WRONG?

Back pain most often comes from the lumbar spine, either at the junction of the fifth lumbar vertebra with the sacrum (known as L5/S1) or one segment above it (L4/5). In the neck, one common area affected is the disc between the lower two cervical vertebrae (C6/7). However, symptoms can originate anywhere in the back, including the thoracic spine and the coccyx. Some people have pain at more than one level.

Pain can be felt in the back itself and/or be referred elsewhere, such as the hand in the case of problems with the cervical spine, and the leg in the case of the lumbar spine (a condition often called sciatica). Or there may be numbness, pins and needles, or weakness. Symptoms in places other than the back may mean that a prolapsed disc is pressing on a nerve root, but this is not necessarily so. Pain in the leg, for instance, can arise because nerves from the same segment of spine go both to the leg and to the part of the back affected.

Discs become less resilient with age, and less easily deformable, which makes 'slipped' discs rare from middle age onwards. But other conditions can cause back pain, including

- narrowing of the disc space
- mechanical strain on the back muscles and ligaments (the commonest condition)
- osteoarthritis (wear and tear) of the spine (including facet joints)
- various types of inflammatory arthritis (e.g. ankylosing spondylitis)
- osteoporosis or thinning of the bones, especially if vertebral fractures result. Most often described in post-menopausal women, osteoporosis occurs in men too
- occasionally, tumours such as secondaries from breast cancer or prostate cancer (anyone who develops significant back pain for the first time after the age of 50 should be examined by their doctor)

Leaving aside the serious causes, which are fewer than 20 per cent of all cases, most episodes of back pain are described as 'mechanical backs'. This means that the cause is thought to be mechanical strain, and implies that it could perhaps have been avoided (see also Chapter 7).

With backs, prevention is better than cure. As orthopaedic surgeons sometimes put it, if back pain has been present less than a month, it always gets better. If it has been there for over 3 months, it never does. This is of course is a parody of the truth, but it underlines the fact that many back problems become chronic.

Many backs are X-rayed if symptoms fail to improve after a few weeks, but with rare exceptions such X-rays tend not to help. Age increases the proportion of X-rays showing degenerative changes, such as disc narrowing and wear and tear, so that by the age of 50 about half of all lumbar spine X-rays show changes, especially in men. But X-ray signs correlate poorly with symptoms, as one should perhaps expect, since muscles and ligaments are not visible on X-ray photographs.

TREATMENT

Treatment for acute mechanical back pain is

- rest, though not for long because muscles become weak. About 24 hours is right for most people
- simple painkillers (ranging from aspirin or paracetamol to analgesics prescribed by your doctor)
- perhaps a little localised heat to relieve muscle spasm in the painful area

Putting a board under the mattress to make the bed harder is often suggested, but this may not help. What back sufferers (present and prospective) need is a supportive mattress as opposed to one which sags. A soft bed may give inadequate support, but so can a hard bed – just feel the unsupported small of your back when you lie on the floor. The ideal (and expensive) mattress is one with pocketed springs.

Some other treatments successfully used for back pain are

- physiotherapy techniques (e.g. traction, mobilisation, short wave diathermy, laser treatment)
- acupuncture
- osteopathy
- chiropractic manipulation
- transcutaneous nerve stimulation (TENS) especially for chronic problems
- injection (e.g. into epidural space or facet joints)

Not all of these are right for everyone. In the case of symptoms from the neck or thoracic spine, many doctors would advise against osteopathic or chiropractic treatment as serious problems have been known to result. When consulting alternative practitioners, it is always important to look for someone reputable.

The single most important approach is to rehabilitate the back. This includes strengthening the muscles, both back and front, and changing the circumstances which led to symptoms in the first place. Back 'classes' or 'schools' run at local hospitals can promote education and self-care and are among the most successful methods of managing back pain.

Without back classes, one can still do a lot. Swimming is a very good form of exercise when recovering from back pain, or when trying to prevent it. The buoyancy of the water takes the body weight, and important muscle groups are exercised. It is not necessary to be a good swimmer, but a reasonable technique is vital – trying to keep your hair out of the water puts unnecessary strain on the neck.

WHO DEVELOPS WORK-RELATED PAIN?

Factors include worker characteristics and workplace characteristics.

- Is your height very different from the average (5'4" for a woman and 5'9" for a man)?
- Are you generally unfit?
- Are you overweight?
- Have you had back trouble in the past?
- Is your back at risk outside work, for example through playing contact sports or at home from caring for a baby?
- Do you smoke? (Nobody knows quite why this matters.)
- Is your work physically heavy?
- Is your job unsatisfying or stressful?
- Do you work long hours (over 50 hours a week)?
- Do you spend much of the day driving?
- Is there vibration from machinery at work?

If two or more of the above statements describe you, then you are at significant risk of getting back pain. However, with some effort all the factors can be changed (except for your height, which can be adjusted for). Chapter 7 covers techniques for lifting, standing and sitting.

CHAPTER SEVEN

The back – reducing the burden

Over a third of accidents (about 50,000 injuries a year) reported to the Health & Safety Executive (HSE) and local authorities arise from lifting or manually handling loads at work. Many sufferers have symptoms in the back, while others have trouble in the hands, arms or other parts of the body.

A single injury can result in days or weeks off work. The HSE quotes an average of 20 days off per injury, which represents a total cost to industry of many millions of pounds.

Not all symptoms can be attributed to one-off incidents. Many are the end-product of repetitive trauma and poor working habits, so these figures are probably a serious underestimate of the situation.

LEGISLATION ON MANUAL HANDLING

There are no legal limits on the size or weight of loads carried at work, but the HSE has drawn up guidelines on lifting. For example, no-one should have to lift a 15 kg weight above elbow height. That assumes the load is easy to grasp and need not be lifted too often (up to 30 times an hour). There are lower weight limits for repetitive lifting and awkwardly shaped packages. The guidelines should not be interpreted too strictly, however, since much depends on workplace routine and individual fitness.

Under the Manual Handling Operations Regulations 1992, the employer has a duty to assess whether the health and safety of employees are at risk from manual handling. This ranges from lifting large loads to transporting hot liquids. The employer must avoid the need for hazardous manual handling where reasonably practicable, and reduce the risk when handling cannot be avoided.

The worker's duties are
● to follow appropriate systems of work
● to use the safety equipment provided
● to cooperate with the employer on health and safety matters

As an employee, you should not have to do your own risk assessment, but your opinion counts and you will often have something important to contribute. Good communications matter, since your employer may be unaware of some aspects of your work unless you speak up. It is in the employer's interest to take notice because safer methods of work are usually more efficient.

MAKING LIFTING SAFE

Ways of reducing the risks associated with manual handling include
● training personnel in manual handling and recognising risk
● changing workplace layout, for instance by removing obstacles
● rethinking work routine, by reducing the size of loads or providing handles
● using more staff
● providing protection, such as gloves or safety boots with steel toe-caps
● providing mechanical aids or introducing new technology, though both of these can involve exposure to new hazards

Lifting a load

Most people know how they should lift something heavy, but tend not to put theory into practice until they have problems, usually back pain.

The essential rules of safe lifting are

● Think first. Do you need to lift it at all? Do you need help?
● Use the right equipment and get enough space around the load.
● Get close to the load and keep your feet apart to create a wide stable base.
● Keep your back straight and bend your knees instead.
● Keep your chin and stomach in.
● Do not twist your body. If you must change angle, move your feet instead.

Symptoms can arise after lifting small weights, and even quite trivial objects. Acute back pain can result from picking up a pen dropped on the floor. This may be because the individual is unfit, has not thought about the need to bend down properly, or has a back which is already compromised, for instance by child-rearing. Even when picking up small objects, get out of your chair and pick them up properly. Instead of twisting or over-reaching

● think BACK
● do not twist
● bend your knees rather than your spine (if your thigh muscles are too weak for you to squat down comfortably, try going down on one knee as a stabiliser)

STANDING

Standing upright puts significantly less weight on the intervertebral discs than lifting, but has its hazards, especially if posture is poor.

When standing, the pelvis should be tilted up slightly and the abdomen tucked in rather than protruding. A glance at those who spend a lot of time standing suggests this type of posture is the exception. Many people stand with an exaggerated curve (or lordosis) of their lumbar spine. This causes a curve of the thoracic spine in the opposite direction, and can precipitate symptoms anywhere in the back.

Poor standing posture is made worse by

- weak muscles (both back and abdominal)
- inappropriate footwear
- the tasks carried out when standing

For instance, work surfaces are often far too low. About a foot below elbow height is optimal for heavy tasks, but it is too low for more delicate manipulations including cooking, using simple controls, and fine work requiring near vision.

Too high a work surface can often be adjusted for, but it is more difficult to correct a surface which is too low. Working on a surface that is too low, for instance writing while standing at a desk, results in the typical 'toothbrushing' posture with the spine slightly bent. Many back sufferers find their symptoms worse when cleaning their teeth, and it is a position best avoided.

Standing can also make legs ache and can worsen foot problems and symptoms of varicose veins. One obvious solution is to provide seating and allow staff to sit or stand as they wish during the day. However, this requires money, at least for some kind of seat and perhaps even for a larger workplace.

As usual, it is the employer's duty to assess risk, but it is also up to employees to think about the work they do and to make the most of any facilities provided. If you think they might not be right for you, say so.

SITTING

The ideal sitting position is comfortable but variable, needing little muscular effort but allowing plenty of free movement. For many sedentary jobs this is obviously not practical, so one has to aim for second best, which is comfortable but more or less constant. This is where good seating and good habits come into their own.

Healthy sitting demands
- seats of the right height and design (see Chapter 2 on ergonomics)
- desks of the right height and size
- work of the right type for the position
- preservation of the curve of the spine (which depends on good posture as well as good seating)

Fidgeting is common, as anyone who has sat in lectures or during a long flight already knows. Seats should be comfortable enough to make fidgeting unnecessary, but fidgeting is better than sitting stock-still in bad seating.

Breaks are important in any kind of deskwork, especially so when using a VDU screen (see Chapter 9). Short breaks every hour are ideal, preferably away from the desk. However, the pressure of work sometimes makes this impossible. If you must stay at your desk, then at least
- lift your eyes away from your work to gaze into the distance
- gently stretch your back muscles
- stretch your arms backwards, upwards and forwards
- keep your neck mobile by gently swivelling from side to side and gently bending from side to side too

CHAPTER EIGHT

Does repetitive strain injury exist?

In 1993, repetitive strain injury (RSI) made headline news when journalist Rafiq Mughal claimed that working with computer keyboards had caused injuries to his upper limbs. Judge Prosser dismissed this, and may have put himself in the history books when he declared that RSI had no place in medical texts. Those forced to give up work because of it were, in his opinion, 'eggshell personalities' who needed to get a grip on themselves.

WHAT IS RSI?

Authorities are divided as to whether RSI exists as a separate condition. Yet the fact that repetitive work with the hands may sometimes cause symptoms should not be disputed. It is well known for instance that telephonists using old-style exchanges were prone to arthritic changes in the finger used for the switches.

One problem is that RSI is a misleading name, since there is no objective evidence of injury or strain, and indeed there may be no objective signs at all. RSI is an umbrella term often used to cover a variety of conditions. Work-related upper limb disorder (WRULD) is a better name, and encapsulates most of what is known about the condition

- the arm or hand is painful or does not function properly
- symptoms are made worse by physical work

Under the heading of WRULD come a variety of specific

conditions such as tenosynovitis (which is a prescribed occupational disease) and carpal tunnel syndrome

Tenosynovitis tends to affect assembly line workers. There is usually pain around the wrist tendons, which is aggravated by movement. Grip is often weak and there may be swelling over the back of the hand or wrist. The characteristic sign is crepitus (an unmistakeable crinkling feel) during tendon movement.

Carpal tunnel syndrome is caused by pressure on the median nerve at the wrist, resulting in tingling and numbness in the fingers, and sometimes visible wasting of muscles at the base of the thumb. The diagnosis can be confirmed by electromyography (EMG). Carpal tunnel syndrome is associated with a number of medical conditions (including hypothyroidism and pregnancy) and, less commonly, with some occupations including butchery, garment working and sheep shearing. A wrist splint helps, though most sufferers need injection into the wrist or an operation to release the nerve from compression.

The controversy and publicity over RSI usually concern those sufferers who do not have either of these two well-defined conditions. Some of them may have pre-existing problems with the neck or arms. It should not surprise anyone if such symptoms worsen with desk or manual work, and perhaps it is unfair to blame employers when this happens.

Symptoms

Most WRULD sufferers do not have neat symptoms and signs and can have any of the following

- pain or ache in the hand, forearm, arm, shoulder or neck
- cramp or a tingling sensation
- swelling, tenderness, weakness, numbness or spontaneous flicking movements

● fewer symptoms when not at work, at least in the early stages

Later, aching can be more persistent, resolving only after weeks of rest, or even longer.

Psychological factors

As with all disorders, WRULD has emotional and social aspects, especially when the sufferer is not believed. Perhaps this is why there is sometimes headache, insomnia, anxiety or depression. Alternatively, perhaps these result from the same work conditions which led to WRULD.

Psychological factors are generally considered important, in that people who are dissatisfied with their work are more likely to develop symptoms of WRULD. But this does not mean that the condition is 'all in the mind'. Just as many sufferers from WRULD become bored and frustrated by having to stop work they enjoy.

WHO GETS RSI?

RSI, as it was then known, became well known in the 1980s, when an apparent epidemic swept Australia and was reported with an enthusiasm resembling mass hysteria. But the condition is much older than that, and may have been known to the papyrus beaters of ancient Egypt.

Nowadays there could be about a million sufferers from it in the UK, according to the RSI Association. Anyone can get it, including poultry packers and pluckers, car workers, checkout operators, Inland Revenue staff and musicians. Although RSI or WRULD has the reputation of being an upwardly mobile disorder with a predilection for journalists, blue collar workers are probably more often affected. The General Municipal Boilermakers union says it has secured more than £1 million in compensation for its members since 1987.

WHAT CAUSES IT?

Prolonged manual work, especially in awkward positions, predisposes to WRULD. Sudden bursts of overwork can precipitate symptoms, as when employees are under pressure to produce more, cover for sick or 'redundant' colleagues, or comply with tight deadlines.

Keyboard workers are known to be at risk under these conditions. Although there is no universally agreed maximum for the rate of work they do, the Health & Safety Executive (HSE) produces guidelines for employers on working conditions which can lead to WRULD. And under the Health and Safety (Display Screen Equipment) Regulations 1992, employers must analyse workstations, assess their risks, and reduce them to the lowest level reasonably practicable. (More about this legislation in Chapter 9.)

COULD YOU BE AT RISK?

See how many of the following apply to you. Are you
● using a lot of force with the arm or hand? ● using the arm in a position that feels awkward or unnatural? ● doing manual work at the wrong height? ● handling tools which are not ideal for the task? ● using equipment designed for someone very different (e.g. much larger or stronger than you)? ● working rapidly to keep up with machinery or work processes? ● working with vibrating equipment? ● working in a cold environment? ● getting few breaks? ● untrained for the job? ● uninformed about possible risks?

If any of these factors apply to you, take action by telling your employer. The remedy may be very simple, for instance a change in the height of a chair. Whatever is required, your employer should take the required action, so talk to your boss or safety officer. Your union representative may also be able to help.

IF YOU HAVE SYMPTOMS OF RSI

See your doctor. Rest helps, at least early on in the condition. You should also tell your employer, since improving working conditions (such as altering seating, workstation, rate of work or daily routine) may be enough to ensure that symptoms improve and stay away.

Work splints for the wrist can help sufferers, especially those doing keyboard work, but they tend to be uncomfortable if worn for long, and some authorities believe they may be damaging in the long term. Splints are impractical for jobs involving food or wetting the hands, although it is sometimes possible to wear rubber gloves over a splint.

There is no proven benefit from steroid injections, anti-inflammatory drugs or surgery, though they have been known to relieve symptoms.

Physiotherapy can be useful. Sometimes psychological help, such as counselling and cognitive therapy, helps sufferers handle their distress.

The legal situation is complex and your trade union should be involved early on. Companies have been successfully taken to court. Compensation awards can be high; Kathleen Harris, an Inland Revenue typist, won a record £79,000. However, some claimants have gained nothing. Whether a claim against an employer will succeed depends on many factors, including the severity of the symptoms, the adequacy of the workstation, staff training, frequency of breaks away from the keyboard, and whether any information on the risks of WRULD was given to the employee. It also depends on the presiding judge.

CHAPTER NINE

VDU hazards and their prevention

Nearly 10 million visual display units (VDUs) are in use in the UK. In some workplaces, computerisation has taken place virtually overnight, with little thought for its impact on working methods. The new technology has brought enormous benefits to businesses, but there is also concern that the paperless office might be hazardous to health.

Repetitive strain injury (RSI) or work-related upper limb disorder (WRULD) is one potential problem (see Chapter 8) and others are discussed below. Some of the adverse effects are unique to the technology, while others are related to the pace of work, the concentration required and prolonged work in a fairly static position.

EYE SYMPTOMS

Prolonged VDU work can make the eyes red and uncomfortable, especially for those who wear contact lens or who already have dry eyes (mostly workers in middle age and beyond). A study from Tokyo shows this is probably because people using VDUs blink less and their tears evaporate more quickly.

Poor images, flickering and bad lighting should be corrected. It also helps to take frequent visual breaks away from the screen and focus on some distant object. Another solution sometimes mentioned is to lower the height of the screen and tilt it upwards, but this is a poor move as far as the neck is concerned.

There is no evidence that VDU work causes long-term eye damage, though it may unmask pre-existing problems. If asked, employers must provide free eye checks to those about to start work with VDUs or those who already use them for a 'significant' part of their work (there is no hard and fast definition of 'significant').

People who wear bifocal spectacles can have problems with VDUs, because when they look at the screen they use the upper (distance) part of their lenses. These people may need different spectacles for work and if so, the employer must provide them. If you want expensive frames, you will probably have to contribute to the cost.

RASHES

Occasionally, VDU users may develop a rash. This is thought to result from the heat of the screen, and in 95 per cent of cases the rash is on the face. It is usually red and itchy, and may also be scaly and greasy, resembling a condition known as seborrhoeic dermatitis (for which mild steroid cream is sometimes needed).

EPILEPSY

It is well known that flickering lights can trigger an epileptic fit in some susceptible people. However, those who have so-called photosensitive epilepsy are few and far between, perhaps one person in every 10,000.

It is not feasible to eliminate screen flicker altogether, though it is possible to reduce it to very low levels. Therefore, epilepsy is not usually a contraindication to VDU work. However if you have epilepsy and are worried about using a VDU, you can contact the Employment Medical Advice Service (via your local Health & Safety Executive office) for further guidance.

RADIATION

VDUs emit small amounts of electromagnetic radiation, some of which is visible (the letters and graphics on the screen), and some invisible. The radiation comprises ultra-violet, infra-red, radiowaves and ionising radiation similar to that of a television screen.

Concern has been voiced over the possible effects of this on the unborn children of pregnant women who use VDUs, in particular the risk of miscarriage and of birth defects. However, several studies have now been carried out which show no increased risk. Since VDU work is usually light office work, it is probably far less of a hazard to pregnancy than heavy manual work.

Despite this reassurance, some women may still worry about it. On the basis that anxiety does pregnant women no good, non-VDU work may on rare occasions be preferable in pregnancy.

NOISE

This is less likely to arise from the VDU itself than from the printer it is connected to. The noise from a printer should not interfere with normal talking or thinking, unless it is meant to act as a warning signal.

Daisy wheel printers are the noisiest. As they are also slow, most offices use laser, dot-matrix or ink-jet printers which happen to be far less disturbing to the ear.

EFFECTS ON THE SPINE

The sitting position puts greater force on the spine than standing, and VDU work, like any intensive desk work, can precipitate back symptoms, especially in those who already have some back trouble, or those who are concentrating too hard to stop.

There are two main ways of preventing problems

● adopting good posture

● taking timely breaks

Many of the measures which prevent back symptoms also help reduce other effects such as stress and WRULD (see the section on preventing problems below).

STRESS

Although individuals vary, headaches and fatigue are the most common symptoms of stress. Many people think eyestrain causes headache; it can do, but it is unusual (if in doubt, ask for an eye check).

Mental fatigue is more often the result of pressurised work and mental concentration. Poor posture also contributes because it puts neck muscles under tension. Another important factor is the isolation associated with computer work. Computer users who were previously sociable clerks or messengers can find office computerisation hard to adapt to.

Handling inadequate software can be very stressful, either when response times are infuriatingly slow, or when the user is struggling with it. Long menus are hard to cope with and should contain seven items or less. Detailed ergonomic standards for software will be produced in the future.

PREVENTING PROBLEMS

Computers should not be introduced where tasks are already being done perfectly well without them. As Bert Lance said, "If it ain't broke, don't fix it".

Mastering a personal computer should include learning to sit at the terminal as well as how to use the software, but it rarely does. The employer has responsibility for reducing the risk from VDU work, although some things you have to do for yourself. See how many of the following measures you can put into action.

● Your chair should be adjustable for height and the back rest for height and tilt. The back rest should give support in the lumbar area (the small of the back), though it should not exaggerate the normal curve of the spine.

● Your chair should tilt slightly forwards, about 5 degrees from the horizontal.

● You should sit symmetrically, facing the keyboard and the screen. Normally, the greater the number of hours spent at a VDU, the greater the risk, but occasional users are sometimes at disproportionate risk because they relegate the keyboard to an unused corner of the desk, and then have to twist to reach it.

● Back, neck and arm symptoms are fewer if the elbows are at 90 degrees and the upper arms vertical when using the keyboard.

● If you have a lot of copy-typing to do, a document holder helps minimise awkward neck movements.

● The desk surface should be large enough, with space to accommodate your forearms in front of the keyboard. The edge of the desk should be smooth.

● There should be enough desk clearance for your thighs, legs and feet.

- Your legs should not dangle. If you are short, you may need a footrest. If you ask for one, your employer must provide it.
- The screen should be separate from the keyboard, and be able to tilt and swivel to suit the user. You should be able to draw a horizontal line between the top edge of the screen and your eyes. Monitor arms are ideal for positioning the screen, but telephone books are better than nothing. Laptop users may find it impossible to get good positioning for the eyes and arms at the same time.
- The screen should be about 60 cm away from your eyes, but this also depends on your eyesight and what is being displayed on the monitor.
- There should be no visible flicker or glare from the screen. Anti-glare attachments are not essential since glare can usually be eliminated with good positioning, at right angles to the window or the strongest light.
- Use a good keyboard technique, touch typing rather than jabbing with one or two fingers.
- Avoid holding the phone between your ear and shoulder and using the VDU at the same time.
- Not everything may yet be known about new technology, so report any adverse effects, whether or not you think they are related to the VDU.

Breaks

However good the workstation and however expert your technique, sitting at the terminal is hard work both mentally and physically. Ideally, no more than half your working day should be at the keyboard.

Breaks should be the order of the day, and taken before fatigue sets in. Short frequent breaks are better than long occasional ones, and are best taken away from the desk, for instance in the cafeteria or in other work, as long as it is not at the VDU.

The pundits recommend a short break every hour, though as many busy employees know this is virtually impossible to a achieve. If pressure of work or intensity of concentration chain you to the desk, then at least

- take your eyes off the screen once in a while to gaze at the distance
- stretch back muscles
- stretch the arms back, upwards and forwards
- keep the neck mobile by swivelling gently from side to side and then bending it from side to side
- flex and extend fingers every so often – do not overstretch them, however, as this can be harmful

LEGISLATION

Following the European Commission Directive 90/270, the Health and Safety (Display Screen Equipment) Regulations 1992 were brought in. The legislation came into effect in January 1993 and covers any employed (including agency temps) and self-employed workers who use VDUs for a 'significant' part of their normal work.

It falls on the employer to

- evaluate possible risks, both physical and mental, from computer workstations
- take steps to reduce them
- plan work so there is variety of activity (but the exact timing of breaks is usually left to the worker)
- arrange eye tests on request and provide spectacles if special ones are needed for the task

- provide information about risks and methods of reducing them
- give health and safety training relevant to VDU use
- ensure that all newly installed workstations comply with minimum requirements. By December 1996, all existing workstations must comply too

The minimum requirements are extensive, they incorporate many of the preventative measures already outlined and include

- the screen must be flicker free to 90 per cent of users
- the screen must swivel and tilt
- the brightness and contrast must be adjustable
- the keyboard must be separate from the screen
- the work surface must be large enough
- any document holders must be stable and adjustable
- the chair should be adjustable in height
- the seat back should be adjustable in height and tilt, though not necessarily independently of the seat
- the workstation must allow adequate clearance for legs
- software must be suitable for the task

CHAPTER TEN

Noise

Many people consider deafness to be an inevitable result of advancing years, but that is not so. Noise at work is the main cause of hearing loss in industrialised countries. The changes normally seen with age may in fact be induced by noise rather than by years, or at least that is what work on primitive tribes suggests. The Mabaan in Sudan, for example, never hear traffic, machinery or gunshot, and their 70 year olds are less hard of hearing than the average 30 year old in the West. But it is debatable how valid such comparisons are.

The history of noise-induced hearing loss goes back about 250 years. In those days, deafness mainly occurred in soldiers in gun battles. Nowadays it more often affects welders, riveters, foundry workers and those who use pneumatic drills. The range of machines used today, together with the size of the workforce, make noise-related problems increasingly important.

The Health & Safety Executive (HSE) estimates that in Britain some 1.7 million people have occupationally related deafness. This is a prescribed industrial disease, for which an employee may succeed in claiming compensation from his employer. Every year, about 1000 new cases successfully win compensation.

WHAT HAPPENS TO THE EAR

Loud noise damages the hair cells of the cochlea. This is the part of the inner ear which turns the vibrations of sound into electrical waves. Noise-induced damage causes, often in this order

1   Tinnitus (ringing in the ears), usually early on. This can be quite disturbing especially when it is severe or occurs in the absence of external sound.

2   Temporary deafness on leaving the noisy area (e.g. after a rock concert).

3   Irreversible and progressive hearing loss.
Deafness is at first worse for high-pitched sounds like S, F or TH. Usual complaints are

● muffled or distorted hearing
● over-sensitivity to loud noise
● trouble using the telephone (because there are no visual clues)
● difficulty talking in pubs and bars (because of the background noise)

The risk of deafness rises with increasing levels of noise. This is measured in decibels (dB), on the so-called A scale which is weighted to make up for the fact that the human ear is more sensitive to high-pitched sound.

The dB scale is logarithmic, so there is a ten-fold increase in sound energy between 80 dB(A) and 90 dB(A), and between 90 dB(A) and 100 dB(A). A quiet library produces just over 20 dB(A), while a pighouse at feeding time gives levels of over 100 dB(A). (These figures, which come from the HSE, are widely quoted in the literature, even though only swineherds can fully appreciate their significance.)

Levels of 80 dB(A) are much the same as those found on a busy street corner and are considered to pose no risk to hearing. But according to the HSE, about 2.4 million workers in Britain are exposed to levels higher than this. Individuals differ in their susceptibility to noise. Problems are thought to start at about 85 dB(A), which is reflected in the Noise at Work Regulations.

LEGISLATION

The 1989 Noise at Work Regulations impose
- a general duty on employers to reduce the risk of hearing loss to the lowest levels practicable
- a specific duty to take action when noise levels are too high (the 'action levels')

Reducing exposure to noise includes measures such as reducing the number of employers working in a noisy area, decreasing the time spend in such areas, acquiring new machinery with built-in noise reduction, and keeping machines in good working order.

There are two action levels, and they are based on noise doses expressed as the Leq. Leq is a measure of exposure to loud noise and takes into account both the intensity and the duration of sound. It is the constant sound level which would give the same amount of energy as the varying level over the working day. For example, 85 dB(A) for 8 hours or 91 dB(A) for 2 hours both give a Leq value of 85 dB(A).

Regulations

Where the daily exposure of an employee is likely to be 85 dB(A), employers have to
- assess the risk by means of a technical noise assessment
- give employees information about the dangers and instruction or training on minimising them
- provide ear protectors to any employee who asks for them
  At 90 dB(A), employers must
- assess risks
- give information and training
- provide ear protectors to all who are exposed, and ensure that they are worn and maintained in good condition
- mark ear protection zones with the right kind of notices

Even though length of exposure to noise is important, everyone who enters these zones, even briefly, must protect their ears.

Sudden blasts of noise, as from explosions, can also be damaging. All the actions needed at 90 dB(A) are also required if the peak sound is at or above 140 dB(A).

EAR PROTECTORS

There are a variety of plugs and muffs available, and all have limitations.

- **Some workers consider them to be inconvenient, uncomfortable or plain wimpish.**
- **They do not entirely cut out noise – especially if they are not used.**
- **Dirty protectors can cause ear infections.**
- **Protectors are generally thought not to jeopardise communications or safety, since sirens and other important signals will usually still be audible. But this may not be the case for workers who already have some hearing loss.**
- **Protectors should really be considered as a second-line measure, although they are sometimes used as a first, or only, resort.**

The employee's role

Under the legislation, employees have duties too. Apart from wearing ear protectors where necessary, they must also use whatever other protective equipment is supplied, such as silencers. You should report any defects to your employer.

RECOGNISING RISK

Factories and farms are not the only noisy workplaces. Excess noise also occurs in offices, either from outside or from within, especially if they are open plan. Specially padded partitions can help reduce noise in open plan offices.

Only accurate noise measurements, with an integrating sound level meter, will show whether there is a noise risk. If you suspect a problem, tell your boss, supervisor or safety representative. Do not be afraid to speak up. You may have noticed something nobody else has.

COULD YOU HAVE A PROBLEM?

- Must you shout to make yourself heard at work?
- Is it hard to hear colleagues when they are about 2 metres away?
- Do your ears ring for no apparent reason?
- Do you have trouble hearing after work?
- Are you hesitant about repeating what you have heard for fear of getting it wrong?
- Do you keep turning the television or radio up?
- Are loud noises painful?

If any of these apply to you, you may be at high risk of noise-induced hearing loss. This is especially so if your out-of-work life is noisy too (see below).

If you already have symptoms when away from work, it may still not be too late. See your doctor or your firm's medical department if there is one. Audiometry (hearing tests) can then be carried out.

Audiometric screening at work is a good idea for noisy workplaces, and some enlightened companies already provide it. The relevant European Commission directive states that employees should be able to have their hearing checked by a doctor, but it does not make audiometry compulsory.

If you are found to be suffering from occupational deafness, you may be entitled to benefit. Ask your local Social Security office and tell your trade union if you have one.

LEISURE NOISE

The hazards of noise are cumulative, so hours of work and length of service matter, and your leisure pursuits pose an added risk. Televisions at full blast can emit well over 80 dB(A) and discos have been estimated to reach 97 dB(A). Disco-goers may not appreciate how loud the sound is, since after a while the noise level appears to fall as the ear gets used to it. In one survey, between 10 and 20 per cent of people going to discos happened to have noisy jobs, so part of the population may be at particular risk.

Tobacco and alcohol may also increase the risk of hearing loss, though this is unproven.

Personal stereos are another hazard.

- Over 5 million people use them in the UK.
- Noise levels easily reach 100 dB(A).
- The volume is often turned up to drown out background noise. Many people travelling on the London underground do this.
- The newer type of earphone that fits inside the ear is especially hazardous because there is little air between speaker and eardrum.
- Young people tend to use personal stereos, and it should be remembered that the risks of noise are cumulative over an individual's lifetime.

NON-AUDITORY EFFECTS OF NOISE

It is a matter of common experience that noise is distracting and makes it difficult to concentrate, and that loud music can interfere with the sense of smell. The non-auditory effects of noise are less well established than the auditory effects, but there is some evidence that loud noise may

- cause disorientation
- increase aggression
- produce feelings of hopelessness
- be linked with learning difficulties
- interfere with colour vision
- increase the incidence of various stress-related disorders, such as migraine, high blood pressure and peptic ulcers. One possible pathway is through raised levels of hormones induced by the stress of loud noise.

CHAPTER ELEVEN

Something in the air

The past few years have seen increasing concern over air pollution, along with a steep rise in the incidence of allergic and respiratory ailments. Asthma now affects an estimated 3 million people in Britain. Doctors report that acute asthma attacks have almost trebled in 11 years. Bronchitis is more common too. Occupational lung diseases, such as asbestosis and coal-workers' pneumoconiosis, are well recognised. It is also reasonable to suppose that air pollution and ill-health are related, even if cast-iron proof is so far lacking.

PASSIVE SMOKING

Of all the modern pollutants, cigarette smoke is the most important, and the easiest to do something about, at least if you are a smoker. A survey carried out by the private health group BUPA and the Confederation of British Industry shows that two-thirds of companies have smoking restrictions agreed with their staff; that leaves a third of companies which do not have any such agreement.

Passive smoking is a special problem in open plan offices and coffee rooms (where the air is sometimes blue with smoke and the walls yellowed by tar). The health effects are difficult to investigate. However, it is easy to see how passive smoking could harm. Smoke contains carbon monoxide along with over 60 other chemicals (including benzene) with the potential to cause cancer.

Passive smoking involves exposure to 'sidestream smoke' (smoke from the lit end of the cigarette, which is unfiltered and therefore higher in harmful chemicals) and 'mainstream smoke' (smoke breathed in and out by the smoker).

The effects of passive smoking at work include

- raising the risk of lung cancer by an estimated 10–30 per cent (passive smoking may be responsible for 300 lung cancer deaths in Britain every year, according to the Independent Scientific Committee on Smoking and Health)
- worsening the symptoms of asthma and bronchitis
- contributing to coronary heart disease (the biggest killer in the UK)
- in women, an increased proportion of low birthweight babies, who are often less resilient to infection
- irritation of eyes, nose, throat and chest
- headaches
- unpleasantly smelly clothes, hair and even paperwork and books
- extreme annoyance to those who have already managed to stop

Are you troubled by passive smoking?

If so, you can become a supporter of ASH (Action on Smoking and Health). This is a highly respected charity which aims to publicise the dangers of smoking and promotes policies to discourage it. You do not have to be a supporter to buy their excellent *Employee's Guide to Clearing the Air* or their *Smoking Policy Manual for Employers*. ASH also runs Workplace Services, a business which helps management to implement non-smoking policies.

NON-SMOKING POLICIES

It is perhaps surprising that tobacco smoke is not covered by the COSHH Regulations 1988 (Control of Substances Hazardous to Health). However, legislation on smoking will be introduced as a result of European Commission directives. By 1996, employers will have to provide at least smoke-free rest areas.

Some companies already have rules on smoking in communal areas (e.g. lifts, lobbies, canteens) or in offices, or permit it only in designated areas and/or at certain times. Others have imposed blanket rulings on smoking on the premises, sometimes introduced as stepwise restrictions. ASH recommends giving employees a notice period of 12 weeks when smoking rules are to change, rather than imposing them overnight.

The benefits of non-smoking policies at work could include ● reduced incidence of diseases related to smoking ● reduced sickness absence ● employer longevity ● higher productivity ● safer premises (smoking is estimated to cause one in eight fires in offices) ● lower insurance premiums (sometimes) ● cleaner environment ● cleaner corporate image

ASH estimates that, all told, the average firm could save £3500 a year per employee by implementing a no smoking policy. The savings may even be greater than this. Under the Health and Safety at Work Act 1974, the employer has a duty to ensure the working environment is safe, so far as is reasonably practicable. To date, this has not been tested in the courts regarding passive smoking. But in 1993, a non-smoking local authority worker called Veronica Bland won £15,000 in an out-of-court settlement for damage alleged to have been caused to her by passive smoking at work. In the USA, a court has ruled that deliberate exposure to tobacco smoke can be deemed to be battery.

A recent report from the Independent Scientific Committee on Smoking and Health recommends that non-smoking should be the norm at work. One reason put forward by firms in defence of allowing smoking is possible resistance (and legal action) by smokers who may consider their rights to have been infringed.

However, smokers are now in a minority; they constitute less than a third of the population. Many smokers would like to stop smoking and even if they do not, can usually see the rationale behind non-smoking policies.

Employees are more likely to accept smoking restrictions at work when policies are introduced as piecemeal changes, and when they are accompanied by programmes to promote good health and give advice and encouragement to help smokers give up the habit. Staff who have opinions on the subject should make management aware of them – dialogue can initiate change.

SICK BUILDING SYNDROME

This is the name given to a group of complaints believed to be caused by indoor pollution. Although recognised by the World Health Organisation, sick building syndrome (SBS) is sometimes less readily accepted by management who may be located elsewhere.

SBS occurs in outbreaks, often in office blocks built in the 1970s that are air-conditioned and hermetically sealed. Over half the staff in a building may be affected. Typically, symptoms occur in a particular building and subside shortly after leaving the premises. They include ● irritation of the eyes, nose and throat ● headache ● fatigue and general malaise ● difficulty concentrating

Symptoms may be minor, but they can have a large impact on sick leave, productivity and employee turnover.

There is some correlation between SBS and passive smoking, but the cause is not really known. Suggested causes are

- volatile hydrocarbons from furnishings and building materials which may set up sensitivity reactions. One such substance is formaldehyde, a known irritant released by urea-formaldehyde insulating foam
- bacteria, fungi and moulds, harboured either by personnel or by cooling systems
- miscellaneous particles, debris or dust (ordinary dust, for instance, is known to dry the skin and irritate the throat)
- house dust mite (known to trigger some cases of asthma)
- lighting, excess noise or VDUs
- low humidity
- high humidity (possibly through growth of bacteria and other microbes)
- psycho-social factors (although there is no evidence for this apart from the observation that women in boring badly paid jobs get symptoms of SBS).

What can be done for sick building syndrome?

Even though the precise cause in unknown, it often helps if the employer remedies faults which can contribute to SBS, such as
- unhygienic or cramped conditions ● poor lighting ● high humidity ● inadequate ventilation

It is not enough just to open windows and leave ventilation to nature. This may reduce the incidence of SBS but can cause other problems, such as exposure to outdoor pollution (e.g. pollen and various oxides of nitrogen from vehicle exhausts), discomfort from draughts, and papers flying off the desk.

HUMIDIFIER FEVER

This is caused by the growth of germs (whether bacteria or amoebae) in the water used to humidify office air. It is easier to treat than SBS and causes different symptoms including fever, malaise, cough and/or breathlessness, tight chest and muscle pains.

Symptoms are invariably worse on Mondays. The cure is to identify the germ in the water reservoir and kill it off. It can be prevented in the first place by using steam humidifiers instead of those using liquid water.

LEGIONNAIRES' DISEASE

This is a type of pneumonia caused by the bacterium *Legionella pneumophila*. Although not necessarily a work-related disorder, it often occurs in workplaces and large institutions because it spreads through contaminated hot water systems or cooling plants and towers.

The Communicable Disease Surveillance Centre records about 200 cases a year in Britain, but there may be many more, especially in fit people who tend to have only mild symptoms.

Older people, especially if they smoke or have a deficient immune system, can get pneumonia with a high fever and may cough up blood. Watery diarrhoea sometimes precedes chest symptoms.

Legionnaires' disease responds to antibiotics (notably erythromycin), but people who have it badly may get severe complications involving the kidneys or bowels, and about 12 per cent die.

ARE YOU SUFFERING FROM INDOOR POLLUTION?

- Do your eyes smart at work?
- Is your nose either blocked or perpetually runny?
- Do you get short of breath on the way to and from work?

● Do you, or others, find your office stuffy?
● Are your business calls punctuated by you coughing or clearing your throat?
● Do you have any symptoms which are worse on Mondays?
● If you do not smoke, do your clothes smell of stale cigarettes after a day's work?
● Do you get frequent throat or chest complaints?
● Are several of your colleagues affected by similar symptoms?
● Is the air-conditioning rarely serviced?

If any of these factors apply to you, you may be affected by indoor pollution.

WHAT YOU CAN DO

1 Share your complaints with colleagues – there could be other sufferers.

2 Your employer must address the problems of air pollution at work, so report them. Managers may not be aware of the problem, perhaps because their offices are elsewhere. Try to give some idea of the extent of the problem, and aim to sound concerned rather than irate.

3 Get the support of your occupational health service if there is one.

4 Tell an Environmental Health Officer or Health & Safety Executive Inspector.

5 Contact your trade union if you have one.

6 If you are ill, see your doctor. Even though there may be no objective abnormality in, for instance, sick building syndrome, it can be important to rule out other conditions.

CHAPTER TWELVE

Accidents

Over the last 30 years, the rate of injury at work has fallen, as has the fatal injury rate (it is now a quarter of what it was 30 years ago). Nevertheless accidents and deaths at work are still significant, especially to those affected.

For 1991/92, the Health and Safety Commission records 170,400 injuries at work and 297 fatalities. This does not include the self-employed, who suffered 3000 injuries and 71 deaths, or the public who suffered 11,100 injuries and 105 deaths. These figures translate into a rate of 1.4 fatalities per 100,000 employees.

The construction industry is associated with relatively high fatal injury rates. In the present economic climate, which favours deregulation, cost-cutting and privatisation, workers in the construction industry may become even more vulnerable.

Most injured employees are men, which reflects on the division of labour between the sexes. However, injuries to women are still substantial. In 1991/2 110,941 men and 34,507 women had injuries which kept them off work for more than 3 days.

Many types of injury occur, and it is obviously possible to suffer more than one type of injury in a single accident for example, when a worker is hit by a vehicle and then trapped beneath it.

Under the Reporting of Injuries, Diseases and Dangerous Occurrences (RIDDOR), which came into effect in 1986, all accidents at work causing death, serious injury or more than 3 days off work must be reported to the Health & Safety Executive

(HSE). 'Close calls' and incidents such as fires, explosions, train crashes and gas escapes, even when no one was hurt, must also be reported to the HSE. In 1991/92, 3676 dangerous occurrences were reported, slightly fewer than in previous years.

It is a criminal offence not to report such occurrences. Even so, there is believed to be substantial under-reporting. One estimate is that two-thirds of incidents may go unreported. Changes in the way accidents (and diseases) are reported may be in the pipeline.

Some incidents are under-reported because they are difficult to recognise. Carbon monoxide poisoning, for instance, may cause lethargy, headache, dizziness, nausea and abdominal pain, especially when it comes on slowly. It has been known for it to be misdiagnosed as flu or gastroenteritis.

WHAT CAUSES ACCIDENTS?

According to some people, the word accident is misleading because it implies that nobody was responsible for what happened, except perhaps fate. In the field of traffic safety, the term accident has been largely replaced by 'crash'. However, its use persists in industry and medicine, even though accidents have causative factors such as

- staffing levels (too low or too high)
- age of the employee (those under 25 and over 50 are more likely to put themselves and others at risk)
- worker motivation
- psychological and social problems
- training and experience
- fitness
- time of day, and possibly time of the month (a higher risk premenstrually has been suggested)

- fatigue and lack of sleep
- drink and drugs
- type of task to be done
- workload (rate of work and number of things to attend to)
- type and design of machinery
- maintenance of plant
- workplace conditions (e.g. lighting)
- emergency procedures
- employer–employee relations

Many mishaps result from an accumulation of factors and a combination of circumstances, each of which might have been trivial had it occurred in isolation.

PREVENTING ACCIDENTS

The HSE estimates that about a quarter of fatal accidents are due to lack of safe systems of work. This may be because they are not provided or because they are ignored. Reducing accidents at work clearly demands more than a haphazard approach and trusting to luck. There are several important measures to be taken in the workplace

- identifying risks, such as dangerous machines or frayed flexes (this is the employer's responsibility and may need the help of an occupational hygienist or an ergonomist)
- controlling known hazards, such as chemicals
- training staff for the job
- reducing risk where appropriate with written instructions or reminders
- providing safety equipment and clothing
- keeping equipment maintained
- ensuring the workplace is clean, uncluttered and unfrenzied
- planning for emergencies (fire drills, emergency exits, first aid)

and rehearsing them well (procedures which can be done easily in everyday situations are harder to get right when panicking)
- looking out for new hazards yet to be identified (for instance, the possible dangers of lasers used in virtual reality)
- ensuring that everyone in the workplace knows that safety is their concern

The right attitude is vital at every level of an organisation. None of the steps mentioned will be of any use if protective clothing is not worn, workers take machine guards off, cleaners unblock vacuum cleaners while they are still plugged in and managers visit factories without wearing the right headgear.

Any business with more than five employees must have, as a minimum, a written safety policy statement. It need not state who is responsible for what, although this is desirable. Many companies, such as large multinationals, do far more than this through company strategies, high profile action plans, and visible involvement at every level. It may be the smaller and medium sized outfits which need it most, but here the safety stance of larger companies can still help, for instance by conducting or funding research into safety, and by requiring contractors working on their behalf to adopt the same stringent standards.

There is a well recognised relationship between minor injuries and more serious injuries requiring time off work. Once a safety culture permeates an establishment, employees become more aware of dangerous circumstances and dubious practises, and report more minor mishaps and near misses. In fact the accident figures may rise once safety is made an issue, but given that under-reporting is probably widespread this is no bad thing.

What can you do as an employee?
- Think SAFETY whenever you do anything.
- Know and use safe systems of work.

- Use equipment properly.
- Refuse to do work for which you have not been trained.
- If you notice any hazards to health or safety, report them promptly to management or your safety officer. This will not brand you a troublemaker, especially if you do it politely.

HAZARDOUS SUBSTANCES

The Control of Substances Hazardous to Health Regulations 1988 (COSHH) came into effect in October 1989. They cover a wide range of substances considered harmful, whether they are in contact with the skin, inhaled or absorbed through the gut or skin. The substances include

- toxic or corrosive substances, such as paints or the chemicals used in dry-cleaning
- pesticides and other agricultural substances
- micro-organisms (bacteria, viruses, fungi) in laboratories
- many dusts
  COSHH requires employers to do the following.

1 Assess the risk to health and any precautions needed.
2 Introduce measures to control or prevent risk.
3 Ensure that measures are used.
4 If necessary, monitor the exposure of workers and carry out surveillance of their health.
5 Inform, instruct and train employees about the risks and the precautions against them.

Sometimes damage only becomes evident many years after exposure. Asbestosis is a classic example of this, although it is not in fact covered by COSHH but by regulations of its own. There may also be other substances, the dangers of which have yet to be appreciated fully. If you are concerned about a particular substance at work, take the matter up with your safety representative, occupational health service or employer.

FIRST AID

Requirements for first aid at work are enshrined in the Health and Safety (First Aid) Regulations 1981, together with the Approved Code of Practice revised in 1990. Every workplace must have a first aid box and one appointed person to take charge of first aid. There must also be notices giving names of first-aiders and location of boxes.

First aid boxes

The contents should be kept free of dust, and the box should be identified with a white cross on a green background, though this is not always adhered to. It should be easily accessible. Names of first-aiders and emergency telephone numbers can be stuck to the lid or door of the box. Among other things, the box should contain

- adhesive dressings in assorted sizes
- two sterile eyepads for injuries
- triangular bandages and safety pins
- sterile dressings in medium, large and extra-large sizes

Many other items, although not specified in the Regulations, can be considered for inclusion in the box:

- disposable gloves
- tweezers
- torch
- notepad and pencil (for recording a casualty's details and progress)
- two plastic bags (Most people know ice is needed for severed digits. In fact the severed part must not touch ice – it should be put in a clean dry plastic bag before being surrounded by ice in an outer bag, and then of course rushed to hospital with the casualty.)

No drugs or potions should be kept in the first aid box. Irrigating solutions for eye injuries, for example, are normally kept on site for immediate use. However, it is a good idea to know where to find simple painkillers, especially aspirin. In the event of a heart attack, one 300 mg tablet of aspirin (chewed) can thin the blood sufficiently to make the difference between life and death. Medical help is still needed urgently, however, and aspirin should not be given to anyone with a peptic ulcer or a history of allergy to aspirin.

First-aiders

Even a low-risk workplace, such as a shop or library, ought to have one first-aider for every 50 employees. This means someone who has had training approved by the HSE for the purpose of the Regulations, and it can be a doctor or nurse who works in occupational health. It is important to have someone physically capable of giving first-aid, as well as able to drop their normal duties immediately in case of an emergency.

In more hazardous workplaces, it is up to the employer to decide whether to provide more than the minimum number of first-aiders.

Where there are particular risks, as on construction sites and in some factories (especially if the local hospital is some way away) the employer may have to provide a first-aid room, regardless of how many employees there are.

The first-aid room should
● be easy for the casualty to get to
● provide somewhere to lie down
● be accessible for ambulance staff who may be carrying a stretcher

It is a good idea for everyone to have some knowledge of first aid, even if there is no statutory requirement for it, because the uninitiated can do more harm than good, especially before the first-aider arrives on the scene. Emergencies can happen anywhere and anytime, for instance while commuting home. Even if the skills are never used, they do increase confidence.

If you are interested in first aid at work, contact the British Red Cross or St John Ambulance (St Andrew's Ambulance Association in Scotland).

HOW DANGEROUS ARE YOU AND YOUR WORKPLACE?

- Are stairs adequately lit – and blown bulbs replaced?
- Have you been trained to operate the equipment you use, even if you only use it occasionally?
- Have you been tempted to carry out repairs yourself?
- Is one drawer in the filing cabinet permanently wonky?
- Are there hazardous substances (known or suspected)?
- Is there loose flooring (tiles, carpet or vinyl)?
- Do flexes trail across the floor?
- Do you know what to do if someone is electrocuted?
- Is your office clean?
- Do you wear long hair or dangling neckchains near machinery?
- Do you always bother with protective gear?
- Do you ever drink before driving or using machinery?
- Do you know how to lift properly? And do you do it?
- Are smoke alarms tested regularly? If so, do you perch on a couple of phone books on a chair to change the batteries?
- Do you wedge fire doors open to ensure fresh air?
- Does your employer know what actually goes on?
- Do you know who is in charge?

CHAPTER THIRTEEN

Getting around

BY CAR

Leaving aside Jonah's journey inside the whale, driving is the most dangerous form of transport. Every week in the UK, about 80 people die after road traffic accidents, and 1200 are seriously injured. The odds are that you will need hospital treatment for an accident for every 20 years that you drive.

Driving is part of many office jobs and often done under pressure. In a day, you may have to drive five hours and fit in nearly a full day's work. According to police statistics, a quarter of motorway accidents are due to fatigue.

Almost all drivers know what they should do, yet once behind the wheel even the most reasonable person can become an aggressive monster who flaunts all the rules. A recent survey reveals that about half of all motorway drivers exceed the speed limit, and 18 per cent of them drive at over 80 m.p.h. Over 20 per cent of drivers killed in accidents have levels of blood alcohol over the legal limit of 80 mg alcohol in 100 ml of blood.

HOW RESPONSIBLE A DRIVER ARE YOU?

1 **I always keep within the speed limit, and drive more slowly in rain**
   a) agree
   b) disagree

---

2 **Police equipment is not that accurate, so I stick to the speed limit plus 10 per cent**
a) agree
b) disagree

3 **In fog, I keep the windscreen wipers going to clear condensation**
a) agree
b) disagree

4 **If I feel tired, I take a break for fresh air and maybe a coffee**
a) agree
b) disagree

5 **I make a point of stopping on long journeys whether I am tired or not**
a) agree
b) disagree

6 **I have a better head for booze than most so I can compensate for having had a couple of drinks with a client**
a) agree
b) disagree

7 **I often have to rummage on the floor or in the glove box for cassettes**
a) agree
b) disagree

8 **The modern motor is very safe so one can afford to take a few risks now and again**
a) agree
b) disagree

9 I keep my car in good condition and check tyre pressures before long journeys
   a) agree
   b) disagree

10 Why bother? I drive a company car. If anything goes wrong I can ring the RAC
   a) agree
   b) disagree

11 Time is money. I'd better press on
   a) agree
   b) disagree

12 This time I am going by rail. It is too far to drive in the time available and I can do some paperwork on the train
   a) agree
   b) disagree

Score

1 a) 0 b) 1	7 a) 1 b) 0
2 a) 1 b) 0	8 a) 1 b) 0
3 a) 0 b) 1	9 a) 0 b) 1
4 a) 0 b) 1	10 a) 1 b) 0
5 a) 0 b) 1	11 a) 1 b) 0
6 a) 1 b) 0	12 a) 0 b) 1

Analysis

Under 5 points: You are a painstaking road user who probably has a full no-claims bonus and a safe future, as long as you watch out for the other guy.

5 to 8 points: You are an average sort of driver. You take a few risks and gets away with it most of the time.

Over 8 points: You fancy your skills behind the wheel, but the truth is that you are something of mobile menace. To keep your licence, you should rethink your attitudes.

In the driving seat

Driving can precipitate or aggravate back and neck symptoms. Avoid hunching over the wheel or bending much at the hips, both of which put stress on the spine. When choosing a car, try to go for a model in which both the height and the angle of the driver's seat are adjustable.

Some manufacturers (e.g. Volvo) also incorporate a lumbar support into the back of the seat. If your car does not have one, a cushion behind the small of the back helps some people. But make sure it does not slip or slide in use as this can be dangerous, especially if you try to re-adjust it while driving.

On car journeys it is worth stopping and getting out of the car occasionally for a good stretch as well as to prevent fatigue. Lone women may be reluctant to stop, and may need to do some forward planning to take their breaks somewhere busy and reasonably safe, like a service area or restaurant.

Drugs

Many drugs affect driving performance. Studies of accidents suggest that 11–20 per cent are associated with the driver having taken a psychoactive drug, such as sedatives or sleeping pills.

Over-the-counter drugs which can affect driving include

- cough mixtures
- cold remedies
- medicines for travel sickness
- antihistamines (taken for hay fever and other allergies)
- some antidiarrhoeals
- some painkillers

Prescribed drugs which can affect driving include

- sedatives
- sleeping pills (remember hangover symptoms the next day)
- some antidepressants

● anticonvulsants
● some painkillers (especially if you take alcohol as well)
● anaesthetics (for 48 hours or so)
● insulin and diabetic tablets
● eyedrops to dilate the pupil

Neither list is exhaustive. If you are not sure about a particular drug, check with your doctor or pharmacist.

Side-effects will be fewer if you stick to the recommended dose. And remember that people differ. It is not always possible to predict an individual's reaction; for example painkillers such as aspirin and codeine make some people drowsy, but not others.

Medical conditions

Only 1 per cent of road accidents are associated with a medical condition. However, many conditions can potentially affect driving, such as ● heart disease ● strokes ● uncontrolled epilepsy ● diabetes ● glaucoma ● any condition requiring an eye patch

It is up to the driver to disclose any mental or physical disability that can affect his or her fitness as a driver, or may affect it in future, by writing to the Drivers Medical Unit at the DVLC (see p.137 for address). More stringent standards apply to commercial drivers and those with a heavy goods vehicle licence.

Alas, not all drivers take this responsibility seriously. A recent study of an outpatient clinic showed that 14 per cent of drivers had inadequate eyesight, but continued to drive, even though many knew they were breaking the law.

If you are not sure whether you need to notify the DVLC, check with your doctor or contact the Driver Medical Unit at Swansea.

Driving in a foreign country

Over half of all medical problems which develop abroad are the result of road accidents. If you drive while abroad on business, bear in mind that

● you may be unfamiliar with the geography, the local road rules (or lack of them) and the type of rental car

● you may be tired or jet-lagged

BY AEROPLANE

Motion sickness

This results from temporary disturbance of the vestibular system (the organ of balance) deep within the ear. Symptoms usually appear in this order

1 Feeling queasy. 2 Going pale and sweaty. 3 Feeling nauseated and light-headed. 4 Vomiting.

There may also be headache and drowsiness. On a turbulent flight, motion sickness is often worsened by fear. It helps to remember that air travel is remarkably safe.

Symptoms are often relieved by fresh air, as on board ship. On a plane or in a car, keep looking out of the window at something like the horizon which is not swaying wildly. Reading or concentrating on something within the cabin makes things worse.

There are many drugs for motion sickness and most cause drowsiness. If you are taking any medications or have glaucoma or prostate trouble, ask your doctor which motion sickness pills will be suitable for you. Other things being equal, match the length of the journey to the duration of action of the drug.

● Short-acting, lasting for about 4 hours (e.g. Kwells or Joy-Rides).

● Medium-acting, lasting for about 8 hours (e.g. Dramamine or Stugeron).

● Long-acting, lasting for 12–72 hours (e.g. Phenergan or Avomine).

Some people get valuable non-drug relief from products like SeaBands and AcuBands which apply pressure to an acupuncture point above the wrist. Scientific proof of their efficacy is lacking but there may be something in it.

Jet-lag

Fairly obviously, jet-lag is due to mismatch between the external (local) time and the normal circadian rhythm of the body clock. Most travellers are familiar with the symptoms, which include

tiredness, drowsiness, disorientation, difficulty concentrating, headache, indigestion and loss of appetite.The body clock is controlled by hormones such as adrenalin and cortisol from the adrenal gland, and melatonin from the pineal, a small gland at the base of the brain. Experimentally, it is possible to reduce jet-lag by taking melatonin capsules at certain times. However, melatonin is not yet available for general use, so other remedies must be used instead.

Physiologists tell us that lighting, meals and other routine activities have an important effect on the body clock, as one might expect. These external cues are known as *zeitgebers* or time-givers.

Without *zeitgebers*, the body follows its own intrinsic rhythm, which happens to be a daily period of 25 hours, not 24 hours. The main implication is that it is easier to shift the body clock backwards instead of forwards, so jet-lag tends to be worse when travelling east. If heading for Australia, gradually delay, not advance, your activities by 12 hours.

Ideally, one should allow a day to adjust to each time zone crossed, but business travellers rarely have that kind of time to spare. Fortunately, simple measures can help.

Before you arrive there are several things you can do to reduce jet-lag.

- On the plane, adjust your watch to the new time.
- Rest as much as possible on the flight, tiredness makes jet-lag worse. Instead of working, try to sleep. It helps if you feel drowsy and here travel sickness pills can work for you. Consider using a short-acting sleeping pill if you have any.
- Avoid dehydration – give the free champagne a miss and aim instead for an average of one soft drink every hour.
- Constipation can also worsen symptoms. Make sure your normal diet provides plenty of fibre.

At your destination *zeitgebers* become especially important, with bright light being the most useful of all. Strong outdoor light is best, but ordinary indoor lighting helps too.

- You can advance your body clock by bright light between 5 a.m. and 11 a.m., for example by being out of doors.
- Similarly, you can delay your body clock by being in strong light between 9 p.m. and 3 a.m.
- Make the most of routines such as meals and baths. Exercise is helpful, and you can combine it with light by taking a brisk walk outside first thing in the morning.
- An electronic device called the Bioclok can help synchronise your activities with time changes. It costs about £49.95 by post from Medical Technology International.
- If your trip is so short that adjusting to local time is out of the question, take your body clock into account. For instance, meetings should be scheduled for the morning (local time) when you are in the USA and for the evening (local time) when in Japan.
- Do not rely on work to keep you awake. A vital meeting increases alertness up to a point and therefore acts as a *zeitgeber*, but it can be a disaster for business.

Other hazards of air travel

There are two golden rules for air travel.

1 Any serious medical condition should be notified to the airline at the time of booking. Make sure you do this even if your secretary handles your travel arrangements.

2 Planes are not ideal places in which to be born or to die. If you are pregnant or unsure whether you are fit to fly, check with your doctor first.

It's also worth remembering

● Pacemakers and artificial joints can interfere with airport security devices.

● Cabin pressure is only about the same as that 6000 feet above sea level. For most people this is perfectly adequate, but the slight lack of oxygen may pose problems for those with asthma, heart disease or anaemia.

● The disparity between cabin pressure and the body can also cause earache or sinus pain, especially if you have had a recent cold, ear infection or sinus trouble. It is a good idea to suck a sweet or chew gum during ascent and descent to reduce the disparity. If you do not have sweets or gum, yawn a few times instead. Both manoeuvres help to keep open the Eustachian tubes that run from the throat to the middle ear and normalise the pressure in the ear.

● Blood flow in the legs can get very sluggish, especially on long flights. Getting up and walking about from time to time helps prevent deep vein thrombosis. When sitting, keep feet moving when you can, and avoid tight socks and crossed legs.

MEDICAL ADVICE FOR FOREIGN TRAVEL

Medical advice for travel to specific countries can be obtained from ● your doctor ● your occupational health department ● Medical Advisory Services for Travellers Abroad ● British Airways travel clinics. Addresses on p.137.

CHAPTER FOURTEEN

Shift work

There are many different shift patterns – from weeks away on an oil platform to a few hours of late evening duty. Night-shifts are the most common type of shift and pose particular problems. However, partial solutions exist.

SO WHAT IS DIFFERENT ABOUT NIGHT-TIME?

The human body is designed to slow down at night. Among the changes which normally take place

- the heart rate drops to its resting level
- breathing slows
- the metabolic rate goes down by 5–25 per cent
- body temperature drops
- levels of the hormones cortisol and adrenalin go down
- levels of growth hormone and prolactin rise

Also, with any luck, we sleep at night. The purpose of sleep is not altogether clear. Physiologists tend to think its function is restoration or preservation of energy, while psychologists are often more fanciful. Adler, for example, considered sleep and dreaming to be problem-solving processes.

Whatever the night is really for, it is clear that expecting the body to work when it is meant to do other things is abnormal.

CONSEQUENCES OF NIGHT WORK

It is more difficult for the body clock to adjust to night work than it is to change a time zone when travelling. This is largely because in night work the external cues (known as *zeitgebers* or time-givers) are working against adapting. The cues include such things as daylight, meals and the fact that almost everyone else is engaged in a different sort of routine. For example, your family are sitting down to breakfast when you are ready for your 'night's' sleep, and the *News at Ten* comes on the television just before you set off for work.

The following problems have been reported in night-workers

- decreased mental powers
- impaired physical performance
- sleepiness at work
- chronic fatigue, whether at work or not
- disruption of family life
- stomach upsets, such as heartburn and indigestion (ulcers too are more common in shift workers)
- painful or irregular periods in women
- higher incidence of cardiovascular disorders, including high blood pressure
- long-term mental problems, such as anxiety
- increased rate of accidents at work

Fortunately hardly anyone has all the symptoms. Many people, about a fifth of the workforce, work a night shift at some stage, in occupations as dissimilar as facial surgery and factory security. Many night workers appreciate the money it can bring in, while some even enjoy the work itself.

SHOULD YOU DO SHIFTWORK?

Night work is particularly hard for the following people to adapt to

- People who revert to a normal diurnal pattern when not working nights, including those (e.g. nurses) who work night shifts some of the time and day shifts the rest of the time

- Workers in middle age and beyond, who may need less sleep than their younger colleagues but are more fussy about when they sleep.
- 'Morning types' who find it hard to sleep by day and stay awake late into the night.
- Parents of young children, because children are noisy and also need continuous attention, preventing the shift worker from sleeping during the day.
- Those with diabetes or other chronic diseases who have to take medicines regularly.

If you fall into any of these categories, perhaps you should seriously reconsider how important it is for you to work at night. As is often the case, parents (usually mothers) of young children can be in a dilemma. Even mediocre childcare costs good money, and the only affordable childcare may be at night, when a partner or other relative can babysit.

Many workers find they have to give up night shifts. If you must work shifts, at least for the time being, then try to minimise the adverse effects of your work.

WHAT CAN BE DONE

You can make the most of work at unsociable hours by concentrating on five areas.

The job itself

Sleepiness tends to peak at around 4 or 5 a.m. Alertness is hard to maintain through the night, especially if your work is repetitive or boring or the shift is very long. It may be possible to reduce the numbers of hours worked at a stretch or to negotiate a change in the nature or variety of the duties (perhaps by swapping with a colleague from time to time).

Failing that, take action when your concentration is flagging. Do not allow yourself to get too comfortable for too long. Try to do something different, such as taking some exercise (walking or just stretching will do). Or splash your face with cold water (especially useful on the forehead and around the eyes). Fresh air is good if you can get it.

If you must sit in front of a control panel or screen, make a conscious effort to take short frequent breaks, say every 20 minutes, just as you would if sitting at a VDU by day. Listening to a radio can help, as long as the music is not too soothing.

If possible, use strong light as a *zeitgeber* to make it seem more like daytime. Obviously there will be no sunlight at this hour, but switch on any strong indoor lighting. In many workplaces at night, lights are cosily dimmed, which increases sleepiness. One option, especially good for occasional night work, is to have a light box or other light system designed to give out around 1000 lux. This is bright enough to prevent drowsiness but not bright enough to change the body clock.

Sleep when working nights

The object is to have sleep which is as near to normal as possible, and to avoid long-term sleep loss which may disrupt family life and make work more difficult.

Make it easier for yourself to fall asleep and stay asleep. You can cultivate the habit of sleeping when it is light, or keep the bedroom quiet, dark and relaxing. You may need, for instance, to move to a back bedroom to escape street noise, and to have dark curtains or dark curtain lining (branches of John Lewis sell curtain lining in a wide variety of colours). You may also sleep more easily if you turn down the heating in the bedroom. If all you can manage is a couple of naps, that is better than nothing.

Learn and use a relaxation technique to help get you off to

sleep, and to make the most of any rest periods even if you are not sleeping.

Train the rest of the family to keep quiet when you are asleep. Since the outside world will never go away, there are limits to what you can achieve. It helps if someone else can answer phone calls, pay the milkman, open the door promptly when the postman brings a parcel, intercept the Avon lady and so on.

On rest days between night shifts try to maintain what you have achieved by staying up late and doing at least some of your sleeping during the day.

Meals

Besides being an important physiological activity, eating is a vital time-keeper too. Shift workers tend to eat badly, which is one possible reason for their higher incidence of stomach complaints, including ulcers. Unfortunately, eating facilities may be poor at work, and night workers often only manage to have meals which are quick and easy to prepare.

The fry-up is typical fare for many shift workers who come in for their main 'evening' meal just as the rest of the family is having breakfast. Many shift workers end up having, in effect, two breakfasts in 24 hours with a stodgy snack at work in between.

Avoiding fatty foods helps prevent indigestion. Try to ensure a varied diet with plenty of fibre, which also counteracts constipation.

Make meals into a social occasion whenever possible, both at home with friends and family and at work with colleagues.

If you suspect your diet is inadequate, take a multivitamin preparation.

Morale

Try to keep up morale by staying positive. Concentrate on the benefits – not always obvious – of night work. For instance, you do not often get stuck in the rush hour, you can shop when the stores are less crowded, and you are around when the kids come in from school so you can enjoy being with them and putting them to bed.

Reward yourself (and your family) for coping, with treats like a bunch of flowers or perhaps the odd meal out. If you are earning more because of night work, try to dedicate part of the money, at least mentally, to something specific (e.g. holidays, school fees, or whatever).

Free time

Try to spend 'quality time' with the family. This may mean making a special effort to play games with the kids and to have sex with your partner (even if it is not at the times you were used to).

Accept that it also needs extra effort to do other things you enjoy, such as seeing friends or going to the pictures – these things are worth it. Also try to get enough exercise.

Keeping up with normal life is essential to mental and physical well-being, but try to stick at least partly to your night-adapted ways.

CHAPTER FIFTEEN

Exercise

If you are like most people, all you exercise is a variety of excuses. Which are your favourites?

EXERCISE EXCUSES

- What can I do? I have arthritis.
- With two young kids, I don't have the time.
- I feel rotten when I exercise so I'm better off the way I am.
- Isn't it a little too late at my time of life?
- By the time I get in from work, the evening's gone.
- I'm hopeless – too uncoordinated for sports.
- Exercise is dangerous. You can drop dead jogging.
- Going to a gym is too much of a palaver.
- My grandpa never did a day's exercise in his life and he lived to a ripe old age.

Analysis

How many of these excuses do you use?

One or two: you are nearly there – all you need is a guiding hand.

Three or four: you may be getting activity and exercise mixed up. In the past, many jobs involved physical exertion. Nowadays machines do much of the work, so we have to make a conscious effort to keep, or get, fit.

> ***Five or six:*** **perhaps you are not aware of all the benefits of exercise, or the fact that it gets easier the more you do.**
>
> ***Seven or more:*** **you are a fairly hardened case, but even so there is hope.**

There are physical hazards from some types of exercise. Some, like jogger's nipple and welly-thrower's finger, are peculiar to particular types of activity. You can drop dead running, or be killed by a passing skateboard, but the risks are far lower if you follow some guidelines

- use the right technique and the right equipment
- work up to any exercise slowly
- do only what is appropriate to your skills and your level of fitness

Of course, you don't have to take up a sport to start getting more physically active. Make it part of your daily routine. You could walk to the station instead of taking the bus; climb the stairs rather than getting the lift. Or take up gardening.

IF YOU HAVE NEVER EXERCISED, HAVE ANY MEDICAL CONDITION, OR ARE WORRIED ABOUT YOUR AGE AND/OR FITNESS, CHECK WITH YOUR DOCTOR BEFORE YOU START EXERCISING.

Even if you have arthritis you can still exercise. It is a question of finding the right activity for you, after consulting your doctor or physiotherapist. Even quite disabled people can exercise usefully, for instance in warm water. For those with arthritis, some local swimming pools offer a regular session from which the general public is excluded.

People who have children or work long hours have a real problem, but it is usually possible to find a compromise. Parents

can look for a leisure centre which provides a crèche, for instance. For a while you may only be able to exercise at weekends, but try to increase your commitment as soon as you can.

So much for the excuses not to exercise. There are many more reasons why one should keep active.

WHY EXERCISE?

In comparison with their sedentary peers, physically fit men and women may be halving their risk of dying at a premature age. Consider what regular physical activity could do for you.

- **Keep your joints supple and muscles strong.**
- **Improve your blood cholesterol level.** While exercise has no discernible impact on total cholesterol, it increases the level of the beneficial fraction of cholesterol (known as HDL-cholesterol or high-density lipoprotein), and thereby reduces the risk of heart disease.
- **Reduce your blood pressure**. Research shows that in some people vigorous physical activity can reduce blood pressure as much as tablets can.
- **Increase your cardiovascular 'fitness'.** Your capacity to do more increases and the risk of heart disease falls. In some circumstances physical activity can even reverse narrowing of the coronary arteries (but please check with your doctor first).
- **Prevent stroke.** A recent study suggests that vigorous regular exercise, preferably started young, may give significant protection against strokes in later life.
- **Prevent osteoporosis (bone thinning).** Regular exercise helps preserve bone density, especially in women after the menopause, when they lose the protective effect of the

hormone oestrogen. The earlier you start, the greater the benefit will be. But active women of all ages between 20 and 80 have denser stronger bones than women who are sedentary.

- **May help to prevent cancer.** Some studies suggest a reduced risk of cancer of the breast and other malignancies, though this is not proven. It may be that physically active people take better care of themselves generally, or perhaps report symptoms sooner.

- **Release encephalins and endorphins.** These are substances produced by the brain which act as 'natural' painkillers and help us cope with minor symptoms and chronic pain. They may also be important in reducing anxiety and in generating the sheer pleasure many people get from exercising.

- **Take your mind off worries and help you relax** and get a good night's sleep. Many studies confirm that those who exercise regularly appear to be less stressed.

- **Keep you slim** by burning calories and building muscle.

- **Help you socialize**, especially if you exercise with family, friends or colleagues.

- **Exercise can prevent you from doing things you ought not to do**, such as spending your Saturday in the pub, or lounging around smoking. New research shows that regular exercise plays a vital role in keeping recent ex-smokers off the weed.

WOMEN AND EXERCISE

Few women take enough physical exercise. There are various reasons for this, not least of which is the fact that sport is less often a part of female culture.

It is vital to make time for exercise in order to do something for yourself and lay down good habits for the future. If you exercise it also acts as a useful role model for others including your family. Exercise will also improve your health. Women benefit even more than men (perhaps twice as much) from taking up exercise.

WHAT IS 'ENOUGH' EXERCISE?

It is no surprise that nowadays doctors 'prescribe' exercise. But, like any other treatment, the dose has to be right. To benefit the heart and other major organs, exercise must

- be brisk
- last for at least 20 minutes
- take place three times a week
- ideally, make use of lots of different muscles

BEFORE YOU START

People sometimes suppose that if something, such as swimming five lengths of the pool, is good for you, then four times as much is four times as good. Of course that is not so, and there are caveats that it is wise to heed.

If you have any of the following, especially if you are over 35 or have never exercised before, CHECK WITH YOUR DOCTOR BEFORE YOU BEGIN EXERCISING

- heart disease
- chest pain
- take regular medication
- diabetes
- arthritis or other conditions
- any doubts about the advisability of exercise

WHAT EXERCISE?

Most forms of exercise can be beneficial, but not all will suit everyone. You can find out more about different sports from The Sports Council (see p.137 for address). Here is a quick run-down of some favourites.

Swimming is an excellent all-round exercise which most people can take up, with lessons if they have never learnt to swim as children. Swimming can be done at your own pace, and the warm moist air surrounding the pool often suits those with asthma who may not be able to do other forms of exercise. This sport is especially helpful for back pain, arthritis and during pregnancy. However, it has not been shown to be of any use in preventing osteoporosis.

Do not try to keep your hair or face dry – this type of swimming technique can create a lot of strain on the joints of the neck. Even when it is done properly, breast stroke can worsen some knee symptoms.

Cycling either on a push-bike or exercise cycle is another sport that can be taken at your own speed. The advantage of an exercise bike is that the weather will not stop you and there is less pollution. You are also less likely to fall over and you do not need a helmet. However, a push-bike is probably more fun. Do not forget to wear reflective clothing at night, and make sure your lights work.

Cycling is a weight-bearing exercise which, done regularly, can help prevent osteoporosis. It also builds up cardiovascular fitness, breathing capacity and strong muscles, especially in the thighs.

Walking is reasonably safe, but you need to do a lot of it to get any benefit. A walk is brisk if, assuming you are fit enough in the first place, it makes you slightly out of breath at the end of it.

Walking can improve posture, but ankle and foot injuries are a risk, so it is important to wear the right shoes.

Jogging is good for increasing stamina, the proviso being that you must definitely be fit before you start. The force of impact of the foot on the ground is many times greater than in walking, so foot and knee injuries are all the more common. Jogging is usually contra-indicated in arthritis, especially if it affects back, hips, knees or feet.

The right footwear is essential. If you must jog after dark, wear something reflective and do not trip over any loose paving slabs or bricks (it has been known).

Aerobics are very good for the cardiovascular system, but those with any medical condition should be especially careful. Sprains and other minor injuries of the ankle, knees and lower back are a risk, though less so with an experienced teacher. Pregnant women and those who have recently had a baby should go very cautiously since their joints are prone to injury, and their abdominal muscles are weak.

Racquet sports such as tennis and squash are popular. They combine many of the benefits of jogging and aerobics, and can be more interesting because they are social activities as well. But they are competitive, which is where problems can arise. Injuries are common, especially when your opponent is fitter or more skilful than you. In squash you should also watch out for eye injuries. Unfit middle-aged players are at particular risk of angina or heart attack, and have been known to collapse after a game, especially if they also have high blood pressure. You should be fit enough before you attempt these sports, and wise enough to know when to stop.

REDUCING THE RISK

As well as heeding the caveats above, you will help avoid problems by following these rules.

- Warm up before exercise and cool down afterwards. The simplest way is a gentle walk, but it does not deal with all the muscles. An alternative is specifically stretching muscles before and after exercise.

- Avoid exercise if your stomach is too full or too empty. A full stomach is bad for digestion, while too little food in the system can lead to a low blood sugar level.

- Make sure you do not run short of fluid. Have enough to drink before and after exercise, especially in hot weather, even if you do not feel thirsty.

HOW BRISKLY?

Other things being equal, use your pulse as a guide to how much exercise you can take.

1 Take your pulse at the wrist, using the forefinger of your other hand over the inner part of the wrist, towards the thumb side. Count the beats for 15 seconds using your watch to time you and multiply by four to get the pulse rate per minute. Your resting (non-exercising) pulse rate gives some idea of your fitness. The normal rate is about 68–76 beats per minute. In general, a lower figure is usual in those who train or do regular sports, while a higher figure suggests lack of fitness (but heart disease and other conditions can also raise or lower heart rate).

2 Subtract your age from 220. This gives you a figure called the age-predicted maximum heart rate. Of course, it takes no account of your fitness, or lack of it.

3　Good brisk exercise means your pulse should reach something like 65–80% of your age-predicted maximum. So if you are 35, your age-predicted maximum is 185, and when exercising you should attain a pulse between 120 and 148 beats per minute. This is your target range. If you are just starting, go for the lower figure at first.

4　Aim to exercise so that you are within your target range for 20 minutes, three times a week. You can exercise more often if you enjoy it, but you do not have to. Three times a week is enough to benefit your health.

Of course, you cannot monitor your pulse continuously throughout exercise without special equipment, but with most types of exercise you can stop at intervals to check your pulse.

Warning – do not 'go for the burn'

Exercise should not hurt. If you develop pain or any other symptoms on exertion, stop right away and check with your doctor. If you have chest pain, and it continues after you stop exercising, get help immediately.

ORGANISED FITNESS

Corporate fitness programmes can be a boon for employees who may not otherwise get around to exercise. Within a firm, they can be integrated into a health promotion package and take in such areas as stopping smoking and sensible drinking.

Corporate programmes also encourage team spirit and help build relationships with colleagues. There is also some evidence that they can help reduce stress at work.

Fitness programmes require space as well as facilities, such as a swimming pool, gym, treadmill, exercise bikes and so on, as well as showers and hairdryers for afterwards. Clearly not every member of staff is at the same level of fitness, so a check by the company doctor often has to be made first, and exercise needs to be graded as well as supervised by a physiotherapist. To date, relatively few firms in Britain have instituted fitness programmes, though they are proving popular with employees in the USA.

In much the same way, general practitioners in Britain are also making use of exercise classes for patients with chronic pain and depression as well as those who are just overweight.

AND FINALLY

Do not think you need to become an elite athlete. In fact it is probably better if you do not. Exercising every day does not necessarily increase your level of fitness, so only do it if you enjoy it. Excessive training can

- predispose to osteoarthritis (or wear and tear of the joints) in later life
- interfere with hormonal metabolism, for instance periods may become scanty or stop altogether
- depress the immune system
- be too time consuming to be compatible with normal life

CHAPTER SIXTEEN

Healthy eating

'You are what you eat', or so it has been said. But what exactly should one eat, and how can it fit in with a busy working life?

The basic nutritional messages are surprisingly simple, though they are not always clear from what is written on the subject. What follows is the logic behind current recommendations.

RULES FOR A HEALTHY DIET

Fruit and vegetables have long-term benefits

The so-called Mediterranean diet includes generous amounts of fruit and vegetables, either raw (but clean), or lightly cooked in a small amount of olive oil, which is low in saturated fats. People in Mediterranean countries tend to eat far more fruit and vegetables than the British. The World Health Organisation recommends even more, about 450 g daily, or an average of five helpings of fruit or vegetables a day (that does not include potatoes).

Several studies show that diets low in fruit and vegetables are associated with an increased risk of lung and other cancers, and we now think we know why. Fruit and vegetables are healthy because they contain anti-oxidants and fibre.

Anti-oxidants have a major role in attacking free radicals, which are toxic molecules that damage DNA and can cause cell mutations, predisposing to cancer and heart disease. Free radicals are incidentally also found in cigarette smoke and barbecued meat.

Anti-oxidants include
- vitamin C
- vitamin E
- beta-carotene (a precursor of vitamin A and even more useful than the vitamin itself since it is only mobilised when body levels are low)
- selenium
- folic acid (particularly important to women in early pregnancy or planning to conceive as it helps prevent spina bifida and other so-called neural tube defects. The recommended dose is 0.4 mg a day)

For almost all vitamins, too much is harmful, and some experts even reckon excess anti-oxidants lower immunity. High levels of vitamin A are particularly harmful, which is why it is probably best to take your anti-oxidants in food.

WHERE ARE ANTI-OXIDANTS FOUND?

Folic acid is found in
- green leafy vegetables (spinach, cabbage, broccoli, sprouts, spring greens)
- root vegetables (carrot, beetroot)
- whole grains
- salmon

Vitamin C is found in
- sprouts, broccoli, peas, green peppers, spring greens
- citrus fruits, blackcurrants, strawberries

Vitamin E is found in
- wheatgerm, whole grains
- nuts

Beta-carotene is found in
- carrots, turnips, yams
- spinach, broccoli, spring greens
- watercress, parsley, tomatoes
- melon, mango, apricots, peaches

Note that lettuce provides few vitamins.

Get clued up on fats

Fatty foods contain a mixture of fats, but often one type predominates. Saturated fats are present in meat fat, dairy fat (e.g. butter and cream) and some blended vegetable oils.

Polyunsaturated and mono-unsaturated fats are believed to be healthier. Polyunsaturated fats are found in
- sunflower oil
- safflower oil
- soya oil
- corn oil
- oily fish
  Mono-unsaturated fat is found in
- olive oil
- peanut oil
- rapeseed oil

Olive oil, which contains about 70 per cent mono-unsaturated fat, may even lower blood levels of low-density lipoprotein (LDL), which is the harmful type of cholesterol.

Not all vegetable oils are low in saturated fats. You need to check the label of oils and margarines, and to bear in mind that heavily hydrogenated fats or oils are saturated.

When reading labels, it is essential to realise that food which is low in cholesterol may not keep the blood cholesterol low. Dietary cholesterol itself is in fact fairly unimportant; it is saturated fat in the diet which turns to cholesterol in the body. Hence a cholesterol-lowering diet is not the same thing as a low-cholesterol diet, an amazing but poorly appreciated fact.

Fibre and starch are healthy

Fibre is essential for a regular bowel habit and may prevent cancer of the colon and other malignancies. It is found in

- flour
- bread (especially wholemeal, also rich in anti-oxidants)
- breakfast cereals
- fruit and vegetables
- pulses and beans
- rice

Wholemeal bread contains about four times as much fibre as white bread, or 9 g per 125 g serving. We should aim to eat 18–20 g of fibre a day, but it is unwise to change suddenly to a fibre-rich diet as you may feel bloated or develop abdominal pain.

High-fibre foods, such as rice, bread, pasta, potatoes and pulses, also contain what are known as complex carbohydrates (or more simply starch). Unlike simple sugars, starch delivers long-lasting energy, athletes often choose pasta as their last meal before a run.

Women need plenty of calcium

A good intake of calcium in youth (age 20–40 years) can help prevent osteoporosis, which affects many women after the menopause. 'Good' means about 1000 mg of calcium a day, or about a pint of milk (700 mg) plus one yoghurt (200 mg). Low fat milk and yoghurt contain just as much calcium as whole milk.

A lot of sugar is unnecessary

Sugar provides energy, but excess sugar can lead to tooth decay and obesity. You may eat more sugar than you realise, especially in biscuits, soups, sauces and cereals. On toast, a yeast extract spread is a healthier alternative to marmalade. If you cannot drink tea and coffee without sugar, use an artificial sweetener.

Be aware of your salt intake

In some people, too much of the sodium present in salt can lead to high blood pressure. Westerners as a rule eat far more salt than necessary, much of it in processed foods, such as smoked and cured meats, sausages, ready-made meals and soups. Check labels for salt under ingredients, or for sodium under nutritional information.

Unless you have high blood pressure, kidney disease or heart failure, you can use salt in cooking (but don't overdo it). At table, however, go easy and taste food before adding salt. You can use less by putting it in a container with smaller holes (e.g. a pepper pot).

Fish can protect against heart disease

Red meat is not all bad. For most people it is an important source of iron. It is the visible fat on meat that is less healthy.

However, fish has some definite benefits. Oily fish in particular contains eicosapentanoic acid (EPA) and other fatty acids, collectively called omega-3 or n-3 polyunsaturated fatty acids. These are believed to be important in reducing the tendency of blood platelets to clot. A study called DART (Diet and Reinfarction Trial) looked at over 2000 men who had had a heart attack and concluded that their risk of death later was 29 per cent lower in those who ate more oily fish.

Eating oily fish, such as salmon, sardines, mackerel, herring, kippers or trout, just twice a week is probably enough to confer benefits. If you eat tinned fish, the oil should be drained off as it is not fish oil.

Opinions on meat differ. Cutting out red meat has been known to relieve the symptoms of arthritis. Vegetarianism has a lot going for it. Vegetarians tend to have lower blood pressures, irrespective of their salt intake, and may even have less heart disease.

Garlic may have special powers

Garlic has been shown in one study to reduce blood cholesterol to a useful extent although there are other studies which do not show this effect. It may also help reduce blood pressure and enable the immune system to work more efficiently.

A little alcohol is probably a good thing

Sensible alcohol intakes are up to 21 units a week for men, and 14 units a week for women, preferably with two or three alcohol-free days a week. One unit equals one pub measure of spirits (in England and Wales), one small glass of sherry, one glass of wine, or half a pint of lager or beer (but extra-strength lager contains nearly three times as much alcohol as the ordinary type).

About 30 per cent of men and 10 per cent of women habitually drink more than this and run the risk of

- social and work problems
- traffic and other accidents
- brain damage or dementia
- cirrhosis of the liver
- higher incidence of cancer of the throat, mouth, gullet, liver, and pancreas
- malnutrition and deficiency diseases (such as beri-beri)
- high blood pressure
- higher risk of heart disease

Some may find this last complication puzzling, since there is evidence that moderate drinking helps prevent heart disease. This is not proven, but seems to be true, especially when the regular tipple is red wine. Grape skin contains phenolic flavonoids which act as anti-oxidants, and apparently some of the components of grape pips may boost the immune system. More work is needed, and so far there is no prescribed dose of alcohol, except that it should be below the recommended limits.

It is hard to stick to a moderate intake when all about you are downing theirs. Thankfully, combining business with booze is much less common than it used to be. Research by the charity Alcohol Concern shows that 40 per cent of businesses now ban drinking during working hours. Many firms are very strict about this, especially if dangerous machinery is used.

For most people, there will still be the odd lunch or dinner, perhaps with clients, at which the drinks will be flowing and there may be the temptation to indulge more than usual to break the ice. Giving alcohol a miss on these occasions can avoid disasters, such as saying yes to a deal when you should be saying no, and making an exhibition of yourself in front of someone important.

If you feel the urge to drink something to slake your thirst or appear sociable, try a low-alcohol drink or mineral water. Or alternate soft drinks with the harder variety.

TWELVE TIPS FOR HEALTHIER EATING

1   Start the day with breakfast. If you include half a grapefruit or banana, you will be on your way to your target of five servings of fruit or vegetables every day.

2   Eat plenty of bread, other cereals and potatoes.

3   Do not miss meals. You may snack on junk food later to make up for it.

4   Choose fish rather than a fatty meat.

5   Make sure you get enough calcium (one pint of milk and one yoghurt daily). This is especially important for women. Low fat dairy products are best.

6   Taste food before adding salt.

7   Acquire a taste for less sugar in tea, coffee and cereals.

8   Have fruit instead of dessert.

9   Watch your drinking.

10 Buy fewer convenience foods. Salads are nature's ready-made meals.

11 Lobby your catering department to offer vegetarian options and to label dishes according to whether they are high or low in saturated fat.

12 Each week, try one new food or dish. Despite swings in nutritional fashion, there are probably no totally bad or good foods. Variety and moderation are the keys to healthy eating.

CHAPTER SEVENTEEN

Pregnancy

Most women are in a position to make up their own minds about working during pregnancy, and it is therefore usually a matter of convenience, finance and personal preference as to low long they carry on. However, there are a few rules concerning hazards.

SOME TOXIC HAZARDS

Under the Control of Lead at Work Regulations 1985, a pregnant woman is not allowed to work with lead. Even when she is not pregnant, acceptable blood lead levels for a woman of reproductive age are lower than those for a man.

Ionizing radiation can affect doctors and those in professions allied to medicine. In pregnant radiographers, for example, exposure to radiation is controlled under the UK Ionizing Radiation Regulations (1985).

A few chemicals, such as the solvent carbon tetrachloride, may be teratogenic (cause birth defects). The risk may persist after birth, especially if the mother is breast-feeding.

You can get more information about these and other hazards from your company doctor, Employment Medical Advisory Service or local Health & Safety Executive. It is obviously preferable to discuss possible hazards with your employer before conception.

Where there are definite risks, pregnant women and those planning to conceive should do one of the following

● limit their exposure to the hazardous substance
● stop work
● change to more suitable tasks

LESS OBVIOUS HAZARDS

There is a possible increased risk of infection from crowded workplaces (such as schools) or from the journey to and from work. Every woman should have been immunised against rubella (German measles) before pregnancy, but there are other infections which may harm the fetus and for which we do not yet have vaccines.

A French study of over 3000 women attempted to define the workplace conditions which might lead to premature labour. Several factors were thought to be important, including

- working standing up for more than 3 hours every day
- carrying loads of over 10 kg
- boring and repetitive tasks
- noisy (over 80 dB for long periods) environments
- very cold or wet workplaces

It follows that heavy or physically demanding work is best abandoned in pregnancy. You probably will not feel like doing it anyway.

Hazards to pregnancy are unfortunately hard to assess, for two reasons. Miscarriage is common, affecting at least one in five pregnancies, and probably many more than that. About 2 per cent of all babies have some kind of congenital abnormality, though often it is only minor. When it happens, it is often impossible to pinpoint the cause. However mothers may feel guilty and wonder where they went wrong.

If the risks at work are unproven, there are no clear guidelines. It depends on the woman and her pregnancy. If you are worried, it may be better for you to be given alternative duties, since fear and worry may themselves be damaging to health.

HOW LONG TO WORK?

Even when all is well, pregnancy takes its toll on the body. Other things being equal, the fitter one is at the start of pregnancy, the longer one can go on enjoying work, assuming the job is suitable.

Unless there are specific hazards or complications, the usual time to start maternity leave is at the 29th week of pregnancy. However, many women want to go on working longer if possible.

Having and caring for a baby is often more taxing than many first-time mothers imagine before the event, though fortunately not as perilous as was thought a generation ago. Some obstetricians still take a gloomy view of pregnant workers, and especially of older pregnant workers (although they are more likely to want to continue working well into pregnancy).

If you would like to go on working beyond 29 weeks of pregnancy, but your midwife, doctor or obstetrician suggest you should stop, it is worth asking why. The answer will tell you whether you are just hearing a well-rehearsed mantra, or whether there are specific reasons which apply to you. You may, for instance, need time off to rest because of

- multiple pregnancy (risk of growth retardation and premature labour)
- threatened miscarriage
- antepartum haemorrhage
- anaemia
- pre-eclampsia (a condition in which there is high blood pressure, protein in the urine, and poor growth of the baby)
- poor fetal movements (this can suggest poor growth)
- pre-existing conditions, such as heart disease, made worse by pregnancy

For those who want to go on working beyond 29 weeks, a reasonable time to stop is at 34–36 weeks. This is what 75 per cent of pregnant women choose to do, preferring to take more maternity leave at home with the baby afterwards.

Factors to consider

- **Do you enjoy work?** Do you need it, either financially or emotionally? If you had to stop, would you get bored?

- **Can you adapt your workplace to your pregnancy?** A growing abdomen needs more room at a desk, for instance, and you also need to be able to keep your legs moving. Good seating is more of a must than ever.

- **What does the job involve?** Physical work and prolonged standing can reduce blood flow through the placenta, though this may not matter if the fetus is growing well. Pregnancy also affects posture. It exaggerates the lumbar curve and can predispose to back trouble. Because of the hormone relaxin, joints are laxer and more prone to damage. It is important to wear suitable shoes (wide enough and flattish) and to avoid heavy lifting.

- **Will you be exposed to smoke or other pollutants?** Passive smoking can cause growth retardation of the fetus.

- **Do you feel up to it mentally?** While most pregnant women function normally, some feel less lucid. There is no known scientific reason for this, though a small survey has recently suggested that pregnancy can cause forgetfulness. In a study of 48 women, 81 per cent judged their memory to be less good than usual, which was confirmed by objective tests. But memory is not everything.

- **Will you find the time and space to put your feet up at work?** Resting with your feet up does more than just prevent ankles swelling, it also increases placental blood flow, which is important if you stay active in late pregnancy.

- **How will you get to work?** Public transport can be especially tiring when carrying a heavy bump. If you can drive instead, your employer may be able to arrange a parking space for you during pregnancy (a doctor's note helps). Or perhaps you could work from home a couple of days a week to reduce the strain.

● **Will you have to go on business trips?** These can be extra tiring. Airlines will be reluctant to let you fly after 32 weeks of pregnancy. If going somewhere tropical, bear in mind that some antimalarial drugs (e.g. mefloquine) are contra-indicated in pregnancy. Malaria itself is a greater hazard during pregnancy because the risk of developing it is higher, and it also poses a danger to the fetus.

● **How long had you thought of working?** As London Transport can confirm, births do occasionally take place in underground train carriages.

● **Should you get some time to yourself before the birth?** This could be in short supply once the baby arrives.

MATERNITY RIGHTS

A pregnant woman's rights cover five main areas.

Time off for antenatal care: a pregnant woman 'should not be reasonably refused' paid time off for antenatal care. This is usually taken to mean antenatal appointments, going for scans and so on, but if you are lucky it may also extend to the grey area of antenatal and parentcraft classes. It is a bad idea to miss these, though, even if you cannot have paid time off for them.

Protection against dismissal: dismissal on the grounds of pregnancy is against the law. It still happens, however, and sporadic cases go to court, often earning the employee large awards (the record so far is £300,000). Incidentally, it is legal to be dismissed during pregnancy on grounds unrelated to pregnancy.

Maternity leave: under the Trade Union Reform and Employment Rights Act (TURERA) 1993, every woman, whether she works full-time or part-time, is entitled to a minimum of 14 weeks paid maternity leave. Many employers offer much more than this.

Maternity pay: the European Commission directive on the Protection of Pregnant Women at Work (92/85/EEC) means increased maternity benefits for women whose babies are due on or after 16 October 1994. From now on, all women who have worked continuously for 6 months or more in the same job will be entitled to statutory maternity pay at 90 per cent of earnings for the first 6 weeks of maternity leave. Lower rates apply to the rest of the leave.

Employment protection: every woman who has worked for 16 or more hours a week in the same job for 2 years or more has the right to return to her job after having a baby. This extends up to 29 weeks after the birth. The job may not be the same job if this is not 'reasonably practicable', but it must not be on less favourable terms than your old job. If for instance any redundancies are made while you are away, a suitable alternative post must be made available for you.

The Maternity Alliance can give you information about your rights (see p.137 for address).

RELATIONS IN THE WORKPLACE

With maternity rights go certain duties. For instance, you must tell your employer in writing when you plan to stop work and later when you plan to return. Your employer must be told about your pregnancy at least 3 weeks before you intend to go on maternity leave. If you do not comply, you could lose your rights to employment protection. You must do this formally even if the firm already knows about the pregnancy, and you must provide a certificate (MAT B1) from your midwife or doctor (check leaflets available from post offices or the Department of Social Security).

If you are unsure about returning to work, it is usually better to keep your options open and say that you intend to return. You will not necessarily know what you want to do until after the baby is born. If you then decide not to return, it will often be easier for your firm to manage than for you to find another post because someone else has taken your old job.

Concealed pregnancies can occasionally run to full term. But do not count on being able to fool colleagues. Even if you want to keep the good news to yourself, the game is likely to be given away by clues such as your increasing girth and 'morning sickness' (especially if it lasts all day).

People can react strangely to a pregnancy at work. Most are helpful and friendly. But some may not be sure how to treat a pregnant colleague, especially when she changes from a career woman into someone who talks nothing but nappies.

Even when she does not change in this way, people sometimes assume that a pregnant woman has only babies on her mind. They can also get very personal. Near strangers may give unsolicited or worrying advice, and almost everyone asks "When is it due?" It is up to you whether to answer personal questions from people you hardly know, and up to you to set the tone of your relationships at work.

CHILDCARE

Good childcare arrangements can take time to organise, so give them some thought early on. Depending on when you are going back to work, you may even want to interview childminders before the baby is born. Or, if this is your second baby, will your current childcare arrangements still work?

Willing relatives, if available, are often the cheapest but not necessarily the best option for childcare.

Childminders stay in their own home and look after your child there. They usually have other children (or their own) as well. Though rates are negotiable, childminders are often the next cheapest form of childcare. They must be registered with Social Services, but if you find someone suitable yourself, you can arrange for Social Services to approve her.

Workplace crèches or nurseries are rarely provided in the UK but usually work out well if you have only one child. As with childminders, problems can arise when your child is too ill to be taken there.

Nannies come into your home and can be qualified (NNEB – Nursery Nurse Education Board) or unqualified. Those who have tried both kinds often prefer the experienced but unqualified variety who may even be willing to fit in some light housework (negotiate this at the interview).

A live-in nanny is usually younger and cheaper, provided you have the room. A daily nanny is popular with professionals who can afford the high rates a good nanny commands. You will not need to change your ways drastically, or make space for her in your home, but, whoever looks after your child, you will have to make space in your life. Some women find it so hard to share their children that they go part-time for this reason alone.

Information on childcare can be obtained from Parents at Work. The Return Consultancy promotes family-friendly initiatives at work and runs pre- and post-maternity workshops to help staff balance family and home life. (See p.137 for addresses.)

CHAPTER EIGHTEEN

Lifestyle evaluation

Overall, is the way you live now likely to be good for your long-term health? This quiz does not pretend to be part of an exact science, but going through the 20 questions should help stimulate further thought and prod you into action.

---

1 Have you been trained for the job you do?
a) yes
b) sort of
c) not at all

2 When lifting an object, do you ask yourself "Do I have to do this? In this way?"
a) usually
b) not often
c) I do not have time to ask myself questions.

3 Do you forgo breaks or habitually work late?

a) no

b) yes

c) only for Brownie points

4 Do you report all accident and injuries, however minor?
a) yes
b) no – it's too wimpish
c) it depends

---

5 Have you become short of breath in the last few years?
   a) no
   b) yes
   c) I have not noticed

6 Have you put on more than one stone in weight since starting your working life (excluding any pregnancies)?
   a) yes
   b) no
   c) never weigh myself

7 Do you take regular exercise?
   a) no
   b) yes, three or more times a week
   c) weekends only

8 Have you had your blood pressure taken recently?
   a) yes
   b) not in the last 5 years
   c) never

9 Have you ever seen your doctor for an illness which could be work-related?
   a) yes
   b) no
   c) not sure – I never mentioned my job

10 Do you think health promotion measures are more important for men or for women?
   a) men
   b) women
   c) both the same

11 Are you now under greater pressure at work than 3 years ago?

a) yes

b) about the same

c) no, much less now

12 Do you suspect your job could be on the line if you put your welfare first?

a) yes

b) no

c) my job is already on the line

13 Do you believe, as some Japanese do, in the concept of karoshi (death from overwork)?

a) no

b) possibly

c) never heard of karoshi before

14 Have you aged less well than friends in other jobs or companies?

a) no

b) yes

c) not sure, I have few friends in other jobs

15 Do you apologise for your mistakes at work?

a) not often

b) yes

c) yes and often for other people's mistakes too

16 When you tell someone off at work do you

a) make sure everyone knows about it

b) tread carefully so as not to damage the working relationship

c) I am the one who always gets told off

17 On holiday, do you take 5 days or more to unwind properly?

a) no

b) yes

c) I cannot remember as far back as my last holiday

18 Do you have a plan for what you want to achieve in 6 months or a year from now?

a) no

b) yes

c) yes and 5 years from now too

19 Do you suspect you are a great employee but a lousy spouse?

a) no

b) yes

c) too late to worry about that now or I have no spouse or partner

20 Are you concerned about missing out on your children?

a) no

b) yes

c) less so now that I work part-time (but there have been sacrifices)

Score

1 a) 0 b) 1 c) 3	11 a) 2 b) 0 c) 1
2 a) 0 b) 1 c) 3	12 a) 2 b) 0 c) 3
3 a) 0 b) 1 c) 2	13 a) 1 b) 0 c) 2
4 a) 0 b) 2 c) 1	14 a) 0 b) 1 c) 2
5 a) 0 b) 2 c) 3	15 a) 1 b) 0 c) 2
6 a) 1 b) 0 c) 1	16 a) 1 b) 0 c) 3
7 a) 2 b) 0 c) 1	17 a) 0 b) 1 c) 2
8 a) 0 b) 1 c) 2	18 a) 1 b) 0 c) 0
9 a) 1 b) 0 c) 2	19 a) 0 b) 1 c) 2
10 a) 2 b) 2 c) 0	20 a) 0 b) 2 c) 1

Analysis

Under 12 points: You are on the right track. Things rarely work out this well without effort, so you can congratulate yourself for taking the trouble.

12 to 29 points: Your life does not seem entirely propitious for your long-term well being. There must be some aspects which you can control or change. If you find that difficult, assertiveness training may help.

30 points or more: Perhaps you are burning the candle at both ends. You need to stop and take stock, even if you happen to take a perverse pleasure in your predicament.

Resources

FURTHER READING

Occupational health
Hunter's Diseases of Occupations (8th ed) by A. Raffle. Edward Arnold, 1994, £145.

Pocket Consultant: Occupational Health (3rd ed) by J.M. Harrington and F.S. Gill. Blackwell, 1992, £17.50.

Lecture Notes on Occupational Medicine (4th ed) by H.A. Waldron. Blackwell, 1990, now out of print.

Ergonomics
Ergonomics, Health and Work by S.T. Pheasant. MacMillan, 1991.

Stress
Life Quality Management – Beating Stress at Work by Anne Woodham. Health Education Authority, 1995, £5.99.

Living with Stress by C.L. Cooper, R.D. Cooper, L.H. Meaker. Penguin, 1988, £5.99.

Attitudes at work
Bullying at Work – How to Confront and Overcome It by Andrea Adams. Virago, 1992, £7.99.

Making Advances – What You Can Do About Sexual *Harassment at Work* by Liz Curtis. BBC Books, 1993, £4.99.

The spine and posture
Looking After Your Back by M.I.V. Jayson. BMJ Publications, 1988, out of print but libraries may have it.

Back Pain: A Handbook for Sufferers by Loci Burn. Hodder & Stoughton, 1993, £4.99.

The Back Book by Maggie Lettvin. Souvenir Press, 1993, £8.99.

Getting around
The Driving Manual from Driving Standards Authority. H.M.S.O., 1994, £8.50

Stay healthy abroad by Rob Ryan. Health Education Authority, 1995, £7.99.

Exercise
Life Quality Management: Staying Fit at Work by Penny Chorlton, Health Education Authority, 1995, £5.99.

The Twelve-Week Executive Health Plan by David Ashton. Kogan Page, 1993, £9.99.

Healthy eating
Life Quality Management: Eating Well at Work by Miriam Polunin. Health Education Authority, 1995, £5.99.

USEFUL ADDRESSES

Occupational health
The Health & Safety Executive (HSE) publishes information for the public on many of the topics in this book, as well as guidance for employers.

HSE Information Centre, Broad Lane, Sheffield S3 7HQ. Tel: 01742 892345.

HSE Books, PO Box 1999, Sudbury, Suffolk CO10 6FS. Tel: 01787 881165. Fax: 01787 313995.

You can get information on Industrial Injuries Disablement Benefit and other benefits from the **Department of Social Security** or the nearest **Citizens' Advice Bureau.**

Ergonomics
The Ergonomics Society can provide a list of professional ergonomists. Write to the Ergonomics Society, Devonshire House, Devonshire Square, Loughborough, Leics LE11 3DW. Tel: 01509 234904.

Stress
Relaxation for Living promotes a holistic approach to stress management. The charity runs correspondence courses in relaxation, sells audio and video tapes, and can provide lists of authorised relaxation teachers in your area. It also arranges seminars and workshops for organisations. Write with a large stamped addressed envelope to 168–170 Oatlands Drive, Weybridge, Surrey KT13 9ET. Tel: 01932 858355.

Attitudes at work
Equal Opportunities Commission, Overseas House, Quay Street, Manchester M3 3HN. Tel: 0161 833 9244.

Commission for Racial Equality, Elliott House, 10–12 Allington Street, London SW1E 5EH. Tel: 0171 828 7022.

Women Against Sexual Harassment, Unit 312, The Chandlery, 50 Westminster Bridge, London SE1 7QY. Tel: 0171 721 7592.

City Centre (can give telephone advice to individuals and companies and will refer you elsewhere if necessary) Sophia House, 32–35 Featherstone Street, London EC1Y 8QX. Tel: 0171 608 1338.

The spine and posture
The National Back Pain Association can give advice and information about many aspects of back pain. The National Back Pain Association, The Old Office Block, 16 Elmtree Road, Teddington, Middx TW11 8ST. Tel: 0181 977 5474.

The Alexander technique is a method of posture control designed to reduce muscular tension and improve body function. It can help prevent back problems. For more information and a list of teachers in your area, contact **The Society of Teachers of the Alexander Technique**, 20 London House, 266 Fulham Road, London SW10 9EL. Tel: 0171 351 0828.

Osteopathic Information Service (gives general information about osteopathy) PO Box 2074, Reading, Berks RG1 4YR. Tel: 01734 512051.

British Chiropractic Association (keeps a register of members) 29 Whitley Street, Reading, Berks RG2 0EG Tel: 01734 757557.

Does repetitive strain injury exist?

RSI Association (a national support group for sufferers). For an information pack, send £3.50 and a 36p stamp to the RSI Association, Chapel House, 152 High Street, Yiewsley, West Drayton, Middx UB7 7BE.

VDU hazards and their prevention

British College of Optometrists (gives guidance on VDUs and the eye) 10 Knaresborough Place, London SW5 0TG. Tel: 0171 835 1302.

London Hazards Centre (a charity which gives advice to workplace and community groups and publishes handbooks on the adverse effects of VDU work, including WRULD) Headland House, 308 Gray's Inn Road, London WC1X 8DS. Tel: 0171 837 5605.

City Centre (gives advice to individuals and trade unionists on office health and safety) see above.

Noise

The **Royal National Institute for Deaf People** (publishes information on noise and hearing loss) 105 Gower Street, London WC1E 6AH. Tel: 0171 387 8033.

Something in the air

Action on Smoking and Health (ASH), 109 Gloucester Place, London W1H 3PH. Tel: 0171 935 3519.

City Centre (issues publications on sick building syndrome and passive smoking) see above.

Accidents

British Red Cross, 163 Eversholt Street, London NW1 1BU. Tel: 0171 388 8777.

St John Ambulance, 1 Grosvenor Crescent, London SW1X 7EF. Tel: 0171 235 5231.

St Andrew's Ambulance Association, 48 Milton Street, Glasgow, G4 0HR, Scotland. Tel: 0141 332 4031.

The Royal Society for the Prevention of Accidents (RoSPA) is Europe's largest safety organisation. It publishes RoSPA Bulletin, the monthly journal *Occupational Health & Safety*, and *WRAP*, a monthly newsheet aimed at employees. It also provides training in avoiding accidents at work, and sells first aid boxes, wallcharts and books. For details, contact RoSPA at Cannon House, The Priory, Queensway, Birmingham B4 6BS. Tel: 0121 200 2461.

Getting around
Drivers Medical Unit, DVLC, Swansea SA99 1TU. Tel: 01792 783686.

Medical Technology International, 36 Victoria Street, Edinburgh, EH1 2JP, Scotland. Tel: 0131 220 4568. Fax: 0130 220 6068.

MASTA (Medical Advisory Services for Travellers Abroad) Tel: 0171 631 4408.

British Airways travel clinics. Tel: 0171 831 5333 (recorded message)

Exercise
The Sports Council, 16 Upper Woburn Place, London WC1H 0QP. Tel: 0171 388 1277.

Pregnancy
The **Maternity Alliance** (can give information about your rights and will send appropriate leaflets if you write with a stamped addressed envelope) 15 Britannia Street, London WC1X 9JP. Tel: 0171 837 1265.

Parents at Work (gives information on childcare and runs a network of local support groups) 77 Holloway Road, London N7 8JZ. Tel: 0171 700 5771.

The Return Consultancy (promotes family-friendly initiatives at work and runs pre- and post-maternity workshops to help staff balance family and home) 33 Lausanne Road, London N8 0HJ. Tel: 0181 986 5105.